Manoel de Oliveira

Contemporary Film Directors

Edited by James Naremore

The Contemporary Film Directors series provides concise, well-written introductions to directors from around the world and from every level of the film industry. Its chief aims are to broaden our awareness of important artists, to give serious critical attention to their work, and to illustrate the variety and vitality of contemporary cinema. Contributors to the series include an array of internationally respected critics and academics. Each volume contains an incisive critical commentary, an informative interview with the director, and a detailed filmography.

A list of books in the series appears at the end of this book.

Manoel de Oliveira

Randal Johnson

**UNIVERSITY
OF
ILLINOIS
PRESS**
URBANA
AND
CHICAGO

Library of Congress Cataloging-in-Publication Data
Library of Congress Cataloging-in-Publication Data
Johnson, Randal, 1948–
Manoel de Oliveira / Randal Johnson.
p.   cm. — (Contemporary film directors)
Filmography: p.
Includes bibliographical references and index.
ISBN-13: 978-0-252-03202-8 (cloth : alk. paper)
ISBN-10: 0-252-03202-0 (cloth : alk. paper)
ISBN-13: 978-0-252-07442-4 (pbk. : alk. paper)
ISBN-10: 0-252-07442-4 (pbk. : alk. paper)
1. Oliveira, Manuel de, 1908—Criticism and interpretation.
I. Title.
PN1998.3.O44J65   2007
791.4302'33092—dc22   2006100921

For Cida, Gabi, and Paul

Contents

My interest in Portuguese cinema, and particularly the films of Manoel de Oliveira, originated in the late 1990s, when I saw, in a very short period of time, three films from different countries that are structured around journeys to or through Portugal: Wim Wenders's *Lisbon Story* (1994), Walter Salles's *Foreign Land* (1995), and Manoel de Oliveira's *Voyage to the Beginning of the World* (1997). These films, made by directors from three different cinematic generations, share a number of features and address similar sets of issues, particularly involving memory, origins, and identity. At the same time, they offer significantly different perspectives on Portugal itself. Piqued in part by these films, I took advantage of a sabbatical quarter to spend the fall of 2002 in Lisbon doing research and screening films with the goal of writing a book on Portuguese cinema, with special emphasis on Portugal's greatest filmmaker, Oliveira. In four months I saw upwards of 130 feature-length films, including all of those by Oliveira, as well as numerous shorts and documentaries. When the opportunity arose to contribute to this series on contemporary film directors, I decided to focus on Oliveira, leaving the broader project for a later date.

This book offers a chronological survey of Oliveira's work, providing at least introductory comments on all of his feature films while recognizing that they warrant more complex and thorough analyses in a broadly comparative perspective. The study would not have been possible without the generous collaboration of many people and institutions in Portugal. First of all, I must thank a number of people at the Cinemateca Portuguesa in Lisbon. It is truly a splendid facility for film research (and not only Portuguese cinema), both at its recently renovated headquarters on Rua Barata Salgueiro in Lisbon and at the Arquivo Nacional das Imagens em Movimento (ANIM; National Archive of Moving Images) in Bucelas. One can only admire the inspired leadership of president João Bénard da Costa and vice president José Manuel Costa. The Cinemateca's staff could not have been more helpful. Specifically, I would like to thank Teresa Borges, Luís Gameiro, Luís Gigante, Sara Moreira, Manuel Mozos, Teresa Tainha, and Joaquim Vacondeus. Special thanks also to José de Matos-Cruz for his meticulous filmographic work, which is an obligatory and rigorously reliable point of departure for research on cinema in Portugal. His *O Cais do Olhar* (1999) served as my guide through Portuguese cinema.

Although the bulk of my research and screenings took place at the Cinemateca, I also screened films at the Instituto do Cinema, Audiovisual, e Multimídia (ICAM; Institute of Film, Audiovisual, and Multimedia) and at Radiotelevisão Portuguesa (RTP). At ICAM, special thanks go to Ana Patrícia Severino, Mário Gabriel Bonito, and Nuno Duarte. At RTP, I am grateful for the assistance of Fernando Alexandre, António Reis, and Maria de Fátima Parente Ribeiro. My contacts at RTP were made possible by José Manuel da Silveira Lopes, to whom I also express my gratitude.

Research for this book was funded by the generous support of a Ben and Rue Pine Travel Fellowship through the UCLA Department of Spanish and Portuguese and the Council on Research of the UCLA Academic Senate. Thanks also to Maria Bolina Lopes, who served as my research assistant on this project.

| | |

Portions of the sections on *Aniki-Bóbó* and *Voyage to the Beginning of the World* appeared in a different form in *The Cinema of Spain and Portugal,* ed. Alberto Mira (London: Wallflower Press, 2005): 40–49, 208–17. At various points in the book I expand on comments first made in "Against the Grain: On the Cinematic Vision of Manoel de Oliveira," *Senses of Cinema* 28 (September–October 2003); www.sensesofcinema .com. Jean A. Gili's interview with Manoel de Oliveira was first published in *Positif* 375–76 (May 1992): 79–84. Ruy Gardnier's interview first appeared in *Contracampo* 66 (November 2004); www.contracampo

.com.br. In the initial reference to a film by Oliveira, I provide the original title followed by a translation in parentheses. Thereafter, I use the English title for those films in U.S. distribution, the original title for all others.

Manoel de Oliveira

Manoel de Oliveira: Talking Pictures |

The Early Years: 1931–65

In September 2004, the Venice International Film Festival presented Lifetime Achievement Awards to American director Stanley Donen (b. 1924) and Portuguese director Manoel de Oliveira (b. 1908). Oliveira's filmmaking career, unsurprisingly, began earlier than that of the younger American director. He made his first film, "Douro, Faina Fluvial" (Labor on the Douro) in 1931 and his first feature, *Aniki-Bóbó*, in 1942, whereas Donen's first feature, *On the Town*, was released in 1949. What may be more surprising for those unfamiliar with the Portuguese director's work is the fact that his career as an active filmmaker has far outlasted that of his American counterpart. Whereas Donen released his twenty-eighth and last theatrical feature, *Blame It on Rio*, in 1984, since that same year—when he turned seventy-six—Oliveira has made twenty-one features, including *O Quinto Império: Ontem como Hoje* (The Fifth Empire: Yesterday as today; 2004), which had its initial screening in the festival that honored the two directors. Oliveira has made a feature film each year since 1990, with the exception of 2001, when he made two. In 2005 he made *Espelho Mágico* (Magic mirror), and in 2006 he completed *Belle Toujours*, both of which had their initial screenings in Venice. It has perhaps become a cliché to say that Oliveira is the world's oldest active filmmaker. But in fact he is.

Oliveira's cinematic longevity, encompassing more than seventy years of activity from the late silent period to the present, is obviously remarkable in its own right. But what is perhaps more impressive is the creative vitality of his films. Unrestrained by the strictures of studio production and commercial imperatives, he has been able to pursue his own vision in a style of his choosing, resulting in films that are original, often provocative, and almost always unorthodox, particularly when measured by Hollywood's standards. In terms of cinematic creativity, he is much younger than many filmmakers half his age.

Highly respected in Europe—particularly in France and Italy—Oliveira's recognition in the United States has been more hesitant. Whereas in Europe he is often acclaimed as a master on the level of Carl Theodor Dreyer, Robert Bresson, Ingmar Bergman, and Roberto Rossellini, in the United States he is sometimes seen as difficult or excessively cerebral. The simultaneous enthusiasm and hesitation may reflect different reactions to the same aspects of Oliveira's work, which is characterized by an iconoclastic reflective and self-reflexive cinematic discourse, with films that are sometimes considerably longer than the norm—almost seven hours, in the case of *Le Soulier de satin* (The satin slipper; 1985)—and a frequently static camera. For those weaned on Hollywood, his films may seem slow, theatrical, or excessively spoken. His themes—which range from frustrated love to questions of nationhood and empire, from configurations of evil to divine grace, from remembrance and aging to relations between art and life—also align his work more with certain philosophical tendencies of European cinema than with standard American fare.

From almost the beginning of his career Oliveira has expressed opposition to conventional forms of cinematic expression driven by commercial imperatives. In 1933 he published a short text titled "O Cinema e o Capital" (Cinema and capital) in which he argues that the commercial orientation of American cinema smothers and subjugates the artist. Rather than bend to commercial demands, he has followed his own path. The same goes for other external demands, such as those of a political nature. When, for example, he released *Benilde ou a Virgem-Mãe* (Benilde or the Virgin-Mother) in the year following the 1974 Revolution in Portugal, the film was accused of being alienated from the country's contemporary sociopolitical reality. Oliveira responded that the film is set in the 1930s, not the 1970s.

The first forty-three years of Oliveira's career—his least productive period—took place under the moralistic and repressive dictatorship known as the Estado Novo, or New State. Censorship was harsh and dissent not tolerated. The notorious political police, the PIDE, were there to silence malcontents. Film-production financing came to be increasingly dependent on the state. Oliveira did not support the Estado Novo, and although he wrote numerous screenplays and treatments during the dictatorship, because of lack of funding he was able to direct only two feature-length films between 1931 and 1963. It was only in the 1970s that he began to direct on a more regular basis.

Oliveira's work has been described as revealing an inclination toward *l'écriture-palimpseste,* or palimpsestic writing, in that his films are often inscribed or constructed on other texts, which are mostly narrative and theatrical (Rollet). Oliveira is most closely associated with three Portuguese writers—Camilo Castelo Branco (1862–90), José Régio (1899–1969), and Agustina Bessa-Luís (b. 1922)—but his filmography also includes versions of writings by Paul Claudel, Madame de Lafayette, and the Jesuit priest António Vieira, among others. All of his films, however, contain significant literary references and allusions. *A Divina Comédia* (The divine comedy; 1991), for example, includes passages or characters from the Bible, José Régio, Dostoevsky, and Nietzsche, although it is not an adaptation, and much less an adaptation of Dante. *O Convento* (The convent; 1995) includes multiple citations from Goethe's *Faust.* *Je rentre à la maison* (I'm going home; 2001) encompasses a staging of a scene from Ionesco's *Exit the King,* another from Shakespeare's *The Tempest,* and a fictitious filming of Joyce's *Ulysses.* In other films references may occupy less space or be more understated, but they permeate his entire body of work.

Through his use of previously existing texts, Oliveira explores the nature of cinematic language, resulting in a concept of film that often goes against commonly held views and practices, such as the ideas that spoken language is a lesser element of the cinema, that the "theatrical," when on screen, is somehow inferior, or that camera movement is essential to cinematic discourse. He has said, somewhat provocatively, that he attempts to make his films as uncinematic as possible and to remove the spectacular and the emotional from his films in order to focus on the ideas and problems involved. Several of his films involve themes that could lend themselves to melodrama, for example, and yet Oliveira studiously avoids melodrama. He has referred to his work as a "cerebral" cinema.

Oliveira also expresses a profoundly ethical posture in his discussion, in multiple films, of art and life, life and death, moral or religious ideals and social reality, good and evil, love and desire, and the possibility of discovering the truth in human beings' enigmatic existence. His films raise many questions, but they rarely provide answers, and they are never prescriptive or didactic. Rather, they present situations involving human conduct on individual, national, and global levels to provoke reflection on the part of the spectator. His cinema is deeply moral, but never moralistic.

To begin to approach Oliveira's view of the cinema, one might consider his appearance in Wim Wenders's *Lisbon Story* (1994), a tribute both to Portugal's capital city and to the cinema. Midway in the film Oliveira appears in a sound studio. Facing the camera and speaking into a microphone, he offers brief comments about God, the universe, humanity, memory, and the cinema: "God exists. He created the universe. . . . We want to imitate God, and that's why there are artists. Artists want to re-create the world as if they were small gods. They constantly think and rethink about history, about life, about things that are happening in the world, or that we think happened because we believe that they did. After all, we believe in memory, because everything has happened . . . but who can guarantee that what we imagine to have happened actually happened? Whom should we ask?" At this point, the film cuts from the studio to a city street and from color to sepia, reminiscent of the cinema's silent period, while Oliveira's words continue in voiceover: "The world, according to this supposition, is an illusion. The only true thing is memory, but memory is an invention. . . . In the cinema, the camera can fix a moment, but that moment has already passed, and the image is a phantasm of that moment; we are no longer certain that the moment existed outside of the film. Or is the film a guarantee of the existence of the moment? I don't know. The more I think about it, the less I know. We live in permanent doubt. Nevertheless, our feet are on the ground, we eat, and we enjoy life."

Oliveira's concerns here involve the ontological status of the image and epistemological questions about the image as a form of knowledge. He does not confuse film and reality, or the cinematic reality—that which we see on screen—with the pro-filmic reality, or that which is placed before the camera. He posits instead the idea of the image as an illusion or a phantasm in its relationship to an objective reality, but also in relation to truth, which is sometimes notoriously difficult to capture. Oliveira's concerns also obviously involve broader moral, existential, or metaphysical questions about human beings in an ultimately enigmatic world, and such questions, generally without answers, arise in multiple ways throughout his work.

Manoel Cândido Pinto de Oliveira was born on 11 December 1908, in the city of Porto, the son of an industrialist, Francisco José Oliveira, and Cândida Ferreira Pinto de Oliveira. His father owned a dry-goods factory in Porto. He also produced the first electric lightbulbs in Portugal, and shortly before his death in 1932 he built an electric energy plant. His son Manoel filmed the plant's inauguration in the short documentary "Hulha Branca, Empresa Hidro-Eléctrica do Rio Ave" (White Coal, hydroelectric company on the Ave River; 1932).

Oliveira's education took place in the Colégio Universal in Porto before he attended a Jesuit boarding school in La Guardia, Galicia.[1] He revealed an early interest in art, and particularly the cinema. In Porto he was able to see German expressionist films produced by Universum Film AG (UFA), Soviet films such as Pudovkin's *Mother* (1926) and Eisenstein's *The General Line* (1929), American films by Chaplin and Griffith, and numerous French and Italian films. He had a special predilection for Max Linder comedies (Andrade, *O Porto* 24–25).

Before making his own films, Oliveira began to make a name for himself because of his athletic prowess. He was a champion pole-vaulter, a competitive diver, and a race-car driver. He even participated in a trapeze act for the Porto Sports Club. His first experience with film came in 1928 when he worked, along with his brother, as an extra in Italian-born Rino Lupo's *Fátima Milagrosa* (Miraculous Fátima). Oliveira also made an appearance in the first sound film made entirely in Portugal, Cottinelli Telmo's *A Canção de Lisboa* (Lisbon song; 1933). He soon moved to the other side of the camera, with only sporadic appearances as an actor after that point.[2]

"Douro, Faina Fluvial"

Oliveira made his first film, the twenty-one-minute "Douro, Faina Fluvial," at the moment of transition between silent and sound cinema. The film deals with diverse work-related activities that take place alongside and in the Douro River in Oliveira's native Porto. "Douro" is not, however, a traditional documentary about the river and the city. Rather, it is much closer to the city symphony films of Walter Ruttmann, Dziga Vertov, Alberto Cavalcânti, and the early Joris Ivens. Antoine de Baecque characterizes the film as a "visual symphony," and José de Matos-Cruz has referred to it as a "geographical mosaic" in which the director brings together a multiplicity of images—often taken from strikingly unusual angles or reflected in the water—of people, boats, trains, barges, bridges, houses, alleyways, ships, light and shadows, crashing waves, objects blowing in the wind, and, above all, the river (Baecque and Parsi 12; Matos-Cruz 73).[3]

According to the director, the idea for the film grew out of an image he saw in a film by Jacques Feyder: the taut chain of an anchored boat resisting the strong currents of a river. The image's power and beauty reminded him of the banks of the Douro, with its intense activity of boats arriving and departing, loading and unloading merchandise. Oliveira apparently had little interest in documentary until he saw Ruttmann's *Berlin: Symphony of a Great City* (1927), which he has referred to as "the most useful lesson in film technique" that he had ever seen ("Manoel" 68). At the same time, he found Ruttmann's film rather cold and mechanical, lacking in a humanity that later films by the German director possessed. Although the modernist age expressed a fascination with machines, it was the humanity that existed along the Douro that interested Oliveira ("Manoel" 67; Baecque and Parsi 95; Andrade *O Porto* 28).

Oliveira has referred to "Douro" as an experiment with cinematic specificity, the multiplicity of perspectives, and with the montage theo-

"Douro, Faina Fluvial" (Cinemateca Portuguesa). |

ries that were circulating at the time (Baecque and Parsi 96). Akin to German expressionism, the film is an exercise in light, shadows, rhythm, and angle, depicting multiple forms of labor associated in some way with the river as well as the urban transformations provoked by the inexorable process of modernization. The key dramatic sequence, in which an oxcart knocks a man down, is provoked when the driver of a car, distracted by an airplane flying overhead, backs into the oxcart, causing the animal to panic. This sequence, one of several fictional moments in the documentary, offers an early indication of the kind of cinematic hybridity that would come to characterize much of Oliveira's work. The film also includes a hint of the self-reflexivity that would become a constant in his films. It opens and closes with an image of the lamp of a lighthouse casting its light as if it were a film projector.

Manoel de Oliveira made "Douro" on a shoestring budget with photographer António Mendes, who could only work on the film during his free time from his day job at a bank. The film was shot on an inexpensive Kinamo camera that Oliveira's father purchased for him, and much of the footage was edited directly on the negative on a pool table in Oliveira's house. The director evokes these circumstances in *Porto da Minha Infância* (Porto of my childhood; 2001). On one of his trips to Lisbon to compete in an athletic event, Oliveira met producer António Lopes Ribeiro, who had seen parts of his film when it was in Lisbon to be developed. Lopes Ribeiro invited him to screen it at the International Congress of Film Critics that was soon to convene in the city. Oliveira rushed to finish the film, and it was screened on 19 September 1931. The Portuguese audience in attendance booed the film, but foreign critics and artists present, such as Luigi Pirandello and Émile Vuillermoz, admired its avant-garde nature. Vuillermoz wrote a very positive review in *Le Temps* (3 October 1931).

The film was also well received by the writers and critics associated with the modernist review *Presença*, which was one of the first Portuguese reviews to see film as art rather than mere entertainment, and particularly José Régio, who would become a close friend and collaborator. Régio noted that Oliveira had achieved something absolutely new in Portugal: the production of a documentary that offers "the powerful vision of a poet" and that "places the spectator in the very center of the frame," drawn in by its vertiginous rhythm. It is a film directed toward "that which is most intimate in our humanity and in our sense of poetry" (*Régio* 15). "Douro, Faina Fluvial" has long since been recognized as a masterpiece of Portuguese cinema.

After the screening of the barely finished film in Lisbon, Oliveira reedited it and added a light musical soundtrack by Luís de Freitas Branco, who came recommended by Lopes Ribeiro. This version was released commercially in 1934 as a complement to Lopes Ribeiro's *Gado Bravo*. In 1994, Oliveira made additional modifications to the film, now with a soundtrack featuring Emmanuel Nunes's "Litanies du Feu et de la Mer No. 2," which is more attuned to the avant-garde impulse of the film than is the music by Freitas Branco.

After "Douro, Faina Fluvial," Oliveira spent a decade only sporadically involved in directorial activities. From 1931 to 1940 he made five short documentaries, but he wrote treatments for a number of potential films, none of which he was able to complete.[4] The documentaries include the above-mentioned "Hulha Branca, Empresa Hidro-Eléctrica do Rio Ave" (1932); "Miramar, Praia das Rosas" (Miramar, beach of roses; 1938), about a coastal town in northern Portugal; "Portugal Já Faz Automóveis" (Portugal now makes automobiles; 1938), which focuses on the country's first automobile plant; and "Famalicão" (1940), on the northern Portuguese city of the same name.

Aniki-Bóbó

Manoel de Oliveira's first feature, *Aniki-Bóbó*, came in 1942. War was raging in much of Europe, and Portugal was entering the second decade of the authoritarian Estado Novo. Not unexpectedly, Portuguese films of the period were well behaved. National cinematic production had averaged fewer than three feature-length films per year since the advent of sound in 1931. They generally fell within a limited number of genres: urban comedies (*A Canção de Lisboa* [dir. Cottinelli Telmo, 1933]; *O Pai Tirano* [dir. António Lopes Ribeiro, 1940]), historical dramas or literary adaptations set in the past (*Bocage—As Três Graças* [dir. Leitão de Barros, 1936]; *As Pupilas do Senhor Reitor* [dir. Leitão de Barros, 1935]), or films with rural settings or that deal with rural characters "displaced" to the city (*Maria Papoila* [dir. Leitão de Barros, 1937]; *A Canção da Terra* [dir. Jorge Brum do Canto, 1938]). None of the films produced during the period openly contradicted the state's ideological designs, although some, such as *A Canção de Lisboa*, poked good-natured fun at the regime.[5] Others were explicitly aligned with it. In 1937, for example, António Lopes Ribeiro, a director and producer closely associated with—and supported by—the Estado Novo, released the propagandistic *A Revolução de Maio*, which was produced by the regime's Secretariado da Propaganda Nacional (Secretariat of National Propaganda) (Pina 81).

On one level, *Aniki-Bóbó* is no exception to this general situation. Its narrative unfolds into a rather conservative stance of reconciliation and moral rectitude. In other ways, however, it stands apart from mainstream Portuguese cinema of the period. It is a film about children, but its major themes and central narrative conflict—a love triangle—are traditionally associated with adults. Oliveira has said that when it was released, the film was criticized for representing children who disobey, lie, and steal. In other words, they act like adults, who sometimes act like children (Baecque and Parsi 135). The film casts authority, and hence authoritarianism, in a sinister light throughout much of the narrative, and it explores in deceptively simple fashion such issues as desire, transgression, guilt, and punishment. In this sense, it is much darker or more "nocturnal" than it appears on first glance (Fonseca, "Aniki-Bóbó"). *Aniki-Bóbó* deals with children's fears in a world in which they appear to be free, but where they are in reality inhibited and constrained by social institutions and expectations.

Given the historical context of its production, *Aniki-Bóbó* can clearly be read in political or sociological terms as a somewhat contradictory exploration of repression and freedom, transgression and punishment. Oliveira has said that his film, shot during the war and the dictatorship, "has a pacifist spirit, even though that was not a direct intention. It spoke against oppression. I included a policeman only because of the film's symbolic aspect. It was an attack on the dictatorship. Police control took the place of an education that should come from civic practice, which did not exist during Salazar's Estado Novo" (Baecque and Parsi 137). A political or sociological interpretation finds resonance in the location shooting along the banks of the Douro River and the use of nonprofessional actors, which have led numerous critics to see the film as a precursor of neorealism. At the same time, its exploration of desire, guilt, and fear lends itself to a psychoanalytical reading, which is bolstered aesthetically by the film's oneiric, frankly expressionist sequences.

Aniki-Bóbó is based loosely on Rodrigo de Freitas's short story "Meninos Milionários," published in *Presença* in 1930. The story focuses on a group of boys within the oppressive space of the classroom, a space they enter only after leaving their freedom and their souls at the door. Oliveira's film takes the core idea of Freitas's story and expands its dramatic elements. It deals with a group of boys—and one girl—who play along the banks of the Douro River in Porto. Its main focus is on two boys, Carlitos (Horácio Silva) and Eduardinho (António Santos), who compete for the attention of Teresinha (Fernanda Matos). Carlitos is shy, distracted, innocent, and naive, whereas Eduardinho, the group's leader, is outgoing, rude, and a bully. After several confrontations with Eduardinho, and in an effort to win Teresinha's favor, Carlitos steals a doll that she has admired in the window of a store called the Loja das Tentações (Shop of Temptations). That night he crawls across rooftops to her window, where he gives it to her.

As the competition between the two boys intensifies, Eduardinho

Carlitos and the doll in *Aniki-Bóbó*
(Cinemateca Portuguesa).

slips and falls down an embankment toward an onrushing train below. Suspecting that Carlitos pushed Eduardinho, the other boys—and Teresinha—turn their backs on him. Abandoned by his friends, Carlitos attempts unsuccessfully to stow away on a boat leaving Porto. Finally, the shopkeeper, who witnessed the accident, clears the air by declaring Carlitos innocent, resulting in his friends' return. Carlitos attempts to return the stolen doll, but the shopkeeper wants him to have it. He again gives it to Teresinha, and the final narrative shot shows the two of them climbing a stairway side by side, each holding one of the doll's hands, while Eduardinho recovers in the hospital.

The boys' drama takes place in interconnected spaces of freedom and repression. The river, the streets, and the nearby hillside overlooking the train tracks represent spaces of freedom where the children swim or play after school. Their freedom in these spaces is only relative, however, since even there they are always under the watchful eye of authority, particularly of the ubiquitous but largely ineffectual policeman and the shopkeeper, who frequently watches them as they walk to school. Perhaps paradoxically, these natural settings give the film a certain level of abstraction and indefinition. The film makes no attempt to reproduce daily life in the city, as a neorealist work might do. The streets are normally empty except for the children and their antagonists (Baecque and Parsi 139).

In sharp contrast to the streets and the river are the school and the home. The school is an institutionalized space of constraint, boredom, and even cruelty. The teacher is stern, humorless, and rigid, and he is given to humiliating his pupils, either by mocking their academic frailties (such as Eduardinho's inability to read fluently) or by sending them to the dunce's corner. It is therefore not surprising that students daydream or allow their attention to wander to the open window, which, as in Freitas's story, represents an outlet to the world of freedom.

The home appears infrequently in *Aniki-Bóbó*, and when it does appear it generally represents a space where children are confined or chastised. It is far from representing a nurturing environment. Significantly, the few adults in the film do not have names, and none of the children's fathers appear; they have been symbolically replaced by representatives of the state and the economy. The mothers who appear are not identified as such. Indeed, the spectator does not even see the face of Carlitos's mother, the only woman to have more than one appearance in the film. The program notes for a 1981 screening of the film in Lisbon suggest that "it's as if growing up were an irreparable loss of identity, an inevitable passage to anonymity. If the passage to the adult world means the loss of a name, and if names say what each thing is, then passage to the adult world also represents a loss of being" ("Aniki-Bóbó").

As its name suggests, the Loja das Tentações, a kind of dry-goods store, represents a space of desire and interdiction because of its possession of items—such as the doll—that are out of the economic reach of the poor children. In many ways, it is the narrative's central focal point, where its conflicts intensify and are resolved. It is a space of transgression and forgiveness. Its window, dominated by the figure of the doll, allows for a double gaze, as the children look in, and the shopkeeper and the doll—the film includes shots from the doll's perspective—look out. Unlike the dour schoolteacher, the shopkeeper is characterized as wise and understanding. He is also the only adult with a sense of humor. He is the one who clarifies the circumstances of Eduardinho's accident, leading to the group's reconciliation with Carlitos, and who provides the film's final explicit message about the futility of anger and conflict. In short, the Loja das Tentações is a space of both sin and redemption.

The love triangle between Eduardinho, Carlitos, and Teresinha plays out against this backdrop through a recurring structure of transgression and punishment. Even the film's title refers implicitly to this structure. "Aniki-Bóbó" is part of a children's rhyme used to determine who will play cops and robbers. As João Lopes suggests, the children's games are forms of initiation into the adult world, a world of law, order, and regimentation (4). The first instance of transgression and punishment occurs in the initial post-credits sequences, when Carlitos's mother helps him dress for school. As she does so, Carlitos plays with a ceramic clown on the dresser and says the words of the rhyme "Aniki-Bóbó." His mother twice tells him to be quiet, and she accidentally knocks his arm into the clown, which falls onto the floor and breaks into many pieces. She flips him on the forehead, complaining about the mess he has made. The fact that he is saying the words to "Aniki-Bóbó" when the clown falls and breaks implicitly introduces the question of good and evil.

After his mother flips him on the head, Carlitos runs out of the room, and an exterior shot shows him coming out of the door and looking up at the sky. He starts to run off to school, but his mother calls him back. He returns hesitantly, fearful of being hit again. In fact, she calls him because he has forgotten a book. She puts it in his book bag, which then becomes the camera's focus. On the bag are written the words "Segue sempre por bom caminho" (Always follow the right path), indicative of the moral strictures presumably guiding society. The words might also be seen as cautionary advice about how to get along under a repressive authoritarian regime.

In the following sequence, Oliveira's good-humored response to this advice reveals that is not always easy to follow the right path, since human nature can take wrong turns, and multiple barriers, temptations, and desires get in the way. As Carlitos runs off distractedly he is almost hit by a truck. He stands in the street looking at it, and he is nearly run over by a car. As he walks along the sidewalk, apparently looking backwards at the car, he runs into a policeman. He continues walking, now looking backwards at the policeman, and he runs into a lamppost. In this comic scene, the truck, the car, the police, and the lamppost all represent obstacles to the "right path." In a broader, more abstract, and perhaps more paradoxical sense, with the exception of the policeman, who is an obvious symbol of authority and potential repression, Carlitos's brief obstacle course is constituted by symbols of modernity: the truck, the car, and the pole of an electric streetlight. In this sense, it recalls the sequence of "Douro, Faina Fluvial," in which an oxcart knocks a man down. Neither instance necessarily represents a critique of modernization; rather, they suggest recognition of the difficulties that the process sometimes entails.

The conflict between Eduardinho and Carlitos intensifies throughout much of the film. On the way to school Carlitos smiles at Teresinha, and a jealous Eduardinho pushes him down into a mud puddle. After school the two of them scuffle by the river, leading Teresinha to console Carlitos because of his black eye. The next day, Carlitos draws a stick figure of a girl on a small blackboard, and Eduardinho hits him with an ink-stained spitball. They later start to fight again, but a passing train distracts them and they run over to a hillside, where Eduardinho trips and falls.

That night, in what has become known as the film's "philosophical sequence," most of the boys sit outside, look up at the stars, and discuss the meaning of life and death. Carlitos is not among them. He is home in bed, trying to sleep, but he has a guilt-ridden nightmare, which Oliveira depicts expressionistically through the superimposition of rapidly changing, recurring images: a swirling vortex, an onrushing train, the doll, the shopkeeper as an ogre, the policeman, Eduardinho, fire, the teacher, Teresinha screaming, the Loja das Tentações, Teresinha beckoning to him with a balloon in hand. His mother awakens him. He had slept in his clothes, and when he gets up and washes, his image is reflected in a broken mirror, his identity shattered. When he goes to school, the boys must write "I will not skip school again," and while the teacher lectures about doing bad deeds, all of the other boys look at Carlitos. It is after this series of events that he attempts unsuccessfully to leave Porto as a stowaway on a boat, while the other boys visit Eduardinho in the hospital.

The shopkeeper clears the air by telling Teresinha that he saw Eduardinho's fall and that it was an accident. Carlitos had nothing to do with it. This leads to reconciliation among the group and to Carlitos's attempt to return the doll. When the shopkeeper tells Carlitos that he can keep it, he provides the film's moral message against anger and violence. The final shot shows that Carlitos finally manages to take Eduard-inho's place beside Teresinha. As Carlitos and Teresinha walk up the stairs holding the doll between them, the camera again providentially tilts toward the sky.

In the end, Carlitos gets to walk beside Teresinha, Teresinha gets the doll, and Eduardinho gets medical treatment. The naive and innocent boy wins out over the unsympathetic bully. After all, as the shopkeeper says, Carlitos has "cleared his conscience" by confessing to his sin, and it seems that he will henceforth "follow the right path." Seen in this way, *Aniki-Bóbó* might, in the final analysis, appear to cede to a form of Christian morality with obvious conservative political implications. Such an interpretation, however, would be precipitous. What about Eduard-inho, who is not blessed with the same good fortune and redemption as Carlitos? He is a bully, and he is very rude to the shopkeeper, but he did not steal from him. Nevertheless, he comes across as an authoritarian figure not unlike the policeman, whereas Carlitos is associated ultimately with the generous, benevolent, and paternalistic shopkeeper. It is perhaps in this sense that Oliveira can correctly assert that *Aniki-Bóbó* offers a critique of Salazar's dictatorship.

Acto da Primavera and "A Caça"

During the decade after *Aniki-Bóbó,* Oliveira worked on several film projects, none of which he was able to bring to fruition. During his years of inactivity, he took care of family businesses, including a vineyard that his wife inherited. In 1952 he wrote a screenplay titled "Angélica," which he submitted to the Fundo de Cinema (Film Fund)—the dictatorship's film-financing mechanism, established in 1948—for possible financing.[6] The film commission sat on the film, not responding one way or another to Oliveira's request. The director has speculated that the lack of a response was a way of keeping him quiet, since he opposed the dictatorship. At the same time, he recognized that for him to reactivate his career he would need to learn more about color, although he already had ample experience as a photographer. Through a friend who represented Agfa in Portugal, he arranged for an internship in Germany, where he studied color photography and cinematography and purchased an Arriflex camera (Baecque and Parsi 143–44, 146).

When he returned to Portugal, Oliveira put what he had learned to use in the twenty-eight-minute documentary "O Pintor e a Cidade" (The painter and the city; 1956), which won an award at the Cork Film Festival in Ireland in 1957. "O Pintor e a Cidade" focuses on the urban aquarelles of António Cruz set against the backdrop of his subject, the city of Porto, which has been important in Oliveira's work from the beginning. It constitutes his first explicit exploration of the kinds of questions about representation that would become so important in his later work. In this case, it is a matter of the relationship between pictorial and cinematic representation as, for example, the film cuts from a painting of an urban landscape to a filmic image of the same landscape or makes a painted train "come alive" by cutting to a "real" train coming out of a station. The truth is that they are both representations; what differs is the mode or mechanism of representation.

Two years later, in 1959, Oliveira made another documentary, "O Pão" (Bread), which was sponsored by the National Federation of the Milling Industry. As the title and its sponsors suggest, the film looks at the industrial process of making bread. But it is not simply a dry, commissioned documentary. Rather, Oliveira sought to give the process a symbolic meaning. To this end, he follows the process from planting, growth, and harvest to milling, baking, and consumption. For José Manuel Costa, "O Pão" is a "multifaceted work, exploding in narrative suggestions and symbols and expressing a universal vision that seeks to encompass everything in one movement—heaven and earth, the sacred and the profane, the country and the city, workers and bosses, labor and leisure, production and commerce, wealth and poverty" ("O Pão").

Oliveira returned to the center of Portugal's film scene in the 1960s with *Acto da Primavera* (Rite of spring; 1963), a work that marks a significant change in the director's trajectory and that initiates some of the cinematic strategies that he would develop more fully in later films. In *Acto da Primavera,* Oliveira offers a version of a popular representation of the Passion of Christ, enacted by members of a rural community in northern Portugal, derived from the *Auto da Paixão de Jesus Cristo* (1559), by Francisco Vaz de Guimarães. He came across the annual Easter drama in the small town of Curalha when he was looking for locations for "O Pão," and he was so taken by it that he wanted to return and register it on film.

Acto has often been referred to as a documentary. While it includes documentary elements, Oliveira did not simply record the popular drama as it took place. Rather, he staged a reenactment in many of the same locales and with the same nonprofessional actors as its "real" representation. In this sense it is a re-presentation of a representation. In documentary fashion, the film includes scenes of townspeople preparing for their roles, shots of flyers announcing the spectacle, and other aspects of the town's daily life. It also inserts additional fictional elements into the narrative, as when a family of middle-class tourists stops to gawk condescendingly at the rural people engaged in their religious reenactment. Oliveira also turns the camera on himself and his small crew as they prepare to film. *Acto* is thus neither exclusively fiction nor documentary, but both at the same time. José Manuel Costa has written that the film's "modernity lies not in the creation of a space between 'documentary' and 'fiction'—as was to a certain extent the case of [Jean] Rouch's 'improvised' or 'spontaneous' fictions—but rather in the exact opposite: the deliberate choice of the *extremes* of these two areas, constructing its essence in the juxtaposition of two *irreducible* zones" ("Acto").

Acto da Primavera (Cinemateca Portuguesa).

According to Costa's interpretation, fiction and documentary do not simply intertwine, as they do to a limited extent in "Douro, Faina Fluvial"; in *Acto da Primavera* they are juxtaposed. The participants in the Passion of Christ are simultaneously themselves—inhabitants of the small town—and actors in the representation. They begin and end the film as townspeople, not as actors. Their costumes, wigs, beards, and "sets" are sometimes awkward, creating a certain distanciation and impeding full spectator identification. The spectator is not unlike the tourists who gawk at their rather primitive, but obviously sincere, efforts.

The film opens with a documentary-like, textual explanation of the *auto,* a medieval theatrical form, and of the director's intentions, indicating that the film is more concerned with expressing the sentiments that gave rise to the representation than in exploring eventual picturesque or anachronistic elements of the drama. The initial post-credits sequence is not of the religious drama but rather of scenes of the town. We see fields, oxen, men and then bulls fighting (establishing conflict as a motif from the outset), men working, young girls running through the town, people fishing in the local river, a man reading the newspaper, and so forth.

The religious drama begins unexpectedly, as, in the midst of these shots of daily life, a girl goes to a well and encounters Jesus. The film then cuts back to the town and reveals the gathering of the spectators, which leads one to believe that the spectacle is about to begin. However, the film cuts not to a stage but to Oliveira and his camera, "the object that will create the second fictitious space, which is a cinematic space" (Costa "Acto"). The focus here is simultaneously on the represented and the representation, the signified and the signifier. This self-reflexive concern with modes of representation constitutes a major strand in Oliveira's oeuvre and a central element in his concept of the cinema.

The end of *Acto da Primavera* again reveals the hybrid nature of Oliveira's cinematic discourse, while at the same time rendering even more explicit and current the motif of conflict evident in some of the film's opening shots. After Christ's crucifixion, his body, wrapped in a white sheet, is placed at the edge of the sepulcher. As one of the Apostles crosses his hands over his chest, the sound of jet fighters is heard on the soundtrack. Documentary shots of violence and war—including shots from Vietnam—begin to alternate with shots of Christ's condemnation and agony. In one shot, Christ's sad face is superimposed over a mushroom cloud. The idea is to draw a sharp contrast between Christ's teachings and the reality of the modern world, as if we were witnessing a descent into hell. The film ends with the suggestion of resurrection implicit in its title: a shot of an almond tree in full bloom, with birds chirping on the soundtrack.

In *Acto da Primavera*, shot two years before Pasolini's *The Gospel According to St. Matthew* (1964), Manoel de Oliveira makes no attempt to impose his own view of Christ or the Passion. Rather, he respects the view held by the townspeople, as expressed in his representation of their pageant. Through the final sequence, however, he does provide an explicit contextualization that will allow the spectator to draw conclusions about the modern world and its distance from the Christian ideal.

Although released after *Acto da Primavera*, the idea for the twenty-minute "A Caça" (The hunt) preceded Oliveira's second feature. Tobis Studios had presented the project to the Fundo de Cinema for funding in 1958, and although Oliveira began filming in 1959, the shooting was interrupted, and he ended up filming part of it simultaneously with his second feature. As he has explained, when the weather was inappropriate for filming *Acto*—that is, when it was overcast—it was good for "A Caça," and vice versa.

"A Caça" tells the story of two idle teenage boys who want to go hunting, but they are unable to obtain a rifle. Instead, they walk off on their own through a marsh. As they walk, they hear the shots of hunters in the distance. At one point they separate, and one of them soon hears the cries of the other: he has fallen into a hole in the marsh and is being sucked down as if it were quicksand. His friend tries unsuccessfully to pull him out and then runs to find help. He tries to flag down a passing train, to no avail. Finally the hunters and some nearby fishermen hear his yells, and they rush to form a human chain to pull the boy out. Unfortunately, the chain breaks, and the men begin to argue among themselves. As the boy is pulled under the muck, the last man holding on to him pleads with the others: "A mão! A mão!" (Give me a hand!). In a darkly ironic image, the arm he holds out has no hand; it is a stump. His plea, as he sinks into the mire himself, is a frantic and vain cry for human solidarity.

The film is permeated with violence and foreboding: images of a fox in a chicken coop, the boys' rather aggressive play, a sequence in a butcher's shop with grotesque images of meat, the violence implicit in the hunt, and so forth. Filmed in a realistic mode with long, horizontal pans and traveling shots—it has been called a fiction film shot in a documentary style—"A Caça" could easily be read as political allegory, an appeal for human solidarity in a moment of crisis, which ties it to the ultimate meaning of *Acto da Primavera,* with its apocalyptic vision of war (Costa, "Manoel" 21).

"A Caça" did have problems with censorship. When Oliveira submitted it to censors in 1963, they gave him an option. He could either change the ending, making it more optimistic, or they would withhold promised funding.[7] He reluctantly agreed, adding a shot in which the boy and his handless helper are saved. This compulsorily modified version circulated from 1963 until 1988. When a series of Portuguese films was organized in Pesaro in 1988, the suggestion was made for Oliveira to re-edit the film, eliminating the imposed ending. He did so, and the film, as he originally intended it, was screened in the Pesaro series. Oliveira maintained the imposed sequence after the new ending with an intertitle identifying it as such. It was not screened in Portugal until 1993 (Fonseca, "A Caça" 1).

Acto da Primavera and "A Caça" are not political films per se, and yet, like *Aniki-Bóbó,* they raise issues—authoritarianism, the violence of the modern world, the need for solidarity—that can be read in political terms, as can several of Oliveira's later films. Nevertheless, it would be a mistake to try to fit the director within a precise political framework. He opposed the dictatorship, but he has never identified with a specific political party or ideology, nor do his films express such a position. Rather, he prefers to cast things in a much broader context, often pointing out, at times with great irony, the contrast between ideals and the reality of human behavior, be it on a personal scale or on the level of nation-states or "civilizations."

After *Acto da Primavera* and "A Caça," Manoel de Oliveira again endured a lengthy hiatus—this time nine years—between feature films. During this period, he directed two short 16mm documentaries, "Villa Verdinho—Uma Aldeia Transmontana" (Villa Verdinho—A village in Trás-os-Montes; 1964) and "As Pinturas do meu Irmão Júlio" (My brother Júlio's paintings; 1965), both of which render homage to friends.

The former portrays diverse aspects of a small town in northern Portugal, with special attention given to the Meneres family. Oliveira has stated that he made it as a gesture of gratitude to Manuel Meneres, whom he had known since the 1930s. In late 1963 Oliveira was arrested by the PIDE, presumably for comments he made during a debate in Porto after a screening of *Acto da Primavera*. Although sick with bronchitis, he was taken into custody and transferred by car from Porto to PIDE headquarters in Lisbon, where he underwent interrogation for his opposition to the regime. Meneres, an influential government supporter, intervened to gain his freedom. Oliveira has noted that Meneres's intervention was an act of courage; others who were in a position to intervene refused to do so (Baecque and Parsi 153–54). "Villa Verdinho" was Oliveira's way of thanking Meneres for his help and support. According to Jacques Parsi, the film belongs to the Meneres family and has never been distributed ("Filmographie" 35–36).

"As Pinturas do meu Irmão Júlio" focuses on the painting of Júlio Maria dos Reis Pereira (1902–83), who is not Oliveira's brother, as the title might suggest, but rather the brother of Oliveira's longtime friend, the writer José Régio. Like Régio, Reis Pereira was a member of the *Presença* group of Portuguese modernism, publishing poetry under the pen name Saúl Dias. With voiceover narration by José Régio and music by the Portuguese guitarist/composer Carlos Paredes (1925–2004), the film makes no attempt to present a visual "catalog" of the painter's work. Rather, by focusing as much on fragments as on entire paintings, Oliveira attempts to provide a sense of the conceptual universe Reis Pereira's art inhabits.

Questions raised in this early period, particularly on the nature of representation and the complexity of human behavior and relations, would continue to inhabit Oliveira's cinematic universe as he shifted directions in the early 1970s. For the first time in his career, which was reaching the forty-year mark, Oliveira would finally attain a certain level of continuity in his work as new possibilities of film financing opened for him, and as his work began to be more widely recognized outside of Portugal.

The Tetralogy of Frustrated Love

O Passado e o Presente (The past and the present; 1971) is the first of four films that have come to be known as the Tetralogy of Frustrated Love, a series that also includes *Benilde ou a Virgem-Mãe* (1975), *Amor de Perdição* (Doomed love; 1978), and *Francisca* (1981). It was this group of films, especially *Amor de Perdição*, that brought Oliveira international acclaim, particularly in Europe (Lemière). The films of the tetralogy have a number of things in common. First, and perhaps most obviously, they all partake in the general, unifying theme of unfulfilled love, which sometimes derives from *amour fou*. Second, although the four narratives take place in different time frames—the early 1970s, the 1930s, the early 1800s, and the mid-1800s—they are all set against the backdrop of a repressive, moralistic society that impedes the characters' fulfillment. Third, they are all based on literary works: the first two on plays, and the last two on novels. Finally, the films consolidate a number of formal traits that run through a large part of Oliveira's work and that begin to articulate his concept of cinematic language: the use of sequence shots and *tableaux vivants*, a theatrical mise-en-scène, an economical use of camera movement, an emphasis on spoken language, a sustained exploration of the relationship between literature, theater, and the cinema, a certain literalness of adaptation, a specific mode of representation by his actors, and a high degree of self-reflexivity.

In the tetralogy, love is a form of obstinate, even obsessive madness that brings characters into conflict with societal or family norms or some kind of constraint. The barrier may be the institution of marriage, as in *O Passado e o Presente,* social, scientific, moral, and religious expectations, as in *Benilde ou a Virgem-Mãe,* feuding families or class differences, as in *Amor de Perdição,* or jealousy, pride, and an obsessive spirit, as in *Francisca.* Although in most instances external factors conspire to thwart their aspirations, social conventions are not the only causes for the characters' frustration. As Jacques Parsi has pointed out, their unyielding love is a kind of "madness of absolute desire" in that the desire itself is more important than the possession ("A trilogia" 74). Because of their obdurate focus, they tend to reject the possible for the impossible, which is what gives their love its value. Vanda, in *O Passado e o Presente,* has a husband by her side, but she prefers a previous spouse who is unreachable. Eduardo offers Benilde a socially acceptable solution, but she rejects it. Simão, in *Amor de Perdição*, could flee with Teresa, but he makes a choice that leads to their permanent separation. José Augusto, in *Francisca*, manages to flee with Fanny but then does not consummate their union. In every case, characters sacrifice the real possibility of love in the name of a distant and ultimately unattainable goal. Their love is often absolute, but it is also doomed almost from the outset, at least in the here and now.

O Passado e o Presente

The first film of the tetralogy, *O Passado e o Presente*, was financed by the Calouste Gulbenkian Foundation in Lisbon in what have become known as the Gulbenkian Years of Portuguese cinema. Luís de Pina has referred to these films as the second phase of Portuguese Cinema Novo (143).[8] In the early 1960s, several young filmmakers—Paulo Rocha, Fernando Lopes, and António de Macedo, among others—joined with producer António da Cunha Telles in an attempt to find new aesthetic solutions for Portuguese cinema, which had become stagnant through the continued repetition of dramatic formulas and stale cinematic conventions. Influenced to a large extent by the French *nouvelle vague*, films such as *Verdes Anos* (Green years; dir. Paulo Rocha, 1963), *Belarmino* (dir. Fernando Lopes, 1964), and *Domingo à Tarde* (Sunday afternoon; dir. António de Macedo, 1965) constituted Portugal's Cinema Novo movement. With their search for different forms of cinematic language, they brought a breath of fresh air to Portuguese cinema.[9] They did not, however, attract a sufficiently large audience to guarantee continuity of production, which is a virtually impossible task in a country with such a small domestic market.

In 1967, filmmakers associated with Cinema Novo joined together in Porto for a Week of New Portuguese Cinema sponsored by the Cineclube do Porto. There they discussed the crisis of Portuguese cinema at the time: "the absence of financial possibilities, the public's lack of interest in the new cinema, the hardening of censorship, . . . the precarious situation of Portuguese cinema in the marketplace, and the decline of the film club movement" (Pina 163). As a result of their discussions, the participating filmmakers sent a report titled "The Profession of Cinema in Portugal" to the foundation, offering a somber diagnosis of the situation and recommending the creation of a Gulbenkian Film Center to finance their projects. The foundation, which had actively supported the arts in Portugal since its inception and provided scholarships for filmmakers and technicians to study abroad, did not accede to the filmmakers' request, but it did establish a program in support of a filmmaking cooperative, the Centro Português de Cinema, which the directors formed at the foundation's suggestion. This arrangement was largely responsible for the best that Portuguese cinema had to offer from 1971 to 1975 (Pina 163–65; Bénard da Costa, *Histórias* 132–42; *O Cinema,* 94–106; Duarte 1–2; "Manoel de Oliveira").

Oliveira's *O Passado e o Presente* was the first film selected for Gulbenkian financing, in part because fellow directors wanted to help him make up for the time lost with extended periods of forced inactivity. The film's premiere was held in the foundation's auditorium in the presence of Portugal's president, Américo Thomaz, and other dignitaries. Based on a relatively little-known three-act play by Vicente Sanches (b. 1936; published in 1964), *O Passado e o Presente* represents a significant departure from Oliveira's previous work. It leaves behind the city of Porto, which had been so prominent in "Douro, Faina Fluvial," and *Aniki-Bóbó,* as well as the popular religiosity of *Acto da Primavera,* to offer an ironic and at times sordid view of Portugal's haute bourgeoisie. A black comedy, or "necrofilm," to borrow João César Monteiro's term (33), *O Passado e o Presente* explores diverse and sometimes perverse aspects of amorous relationships and the institution of marriage.

O Passado e o Presente tells the story of Vanda (Maria de Saisset), who is married to Firmino (Pedro Pinheiro) but has a pathological adoration for her first husband, Ricardo (Alberto Inácio), who was killed in an automobile accident. Although she did not get along with Ricardo when he was alive, her mansion is filled with photographs of him, as if shrines to the dead. Meanwhile, she treats Firmino with derision and ridicule. In other words, she loves the past more than the present, the unattainable deceased husband more than the flesh-and-blood one at her side. Ricardo's identical-twin brother, Daniel (played by the same actor), is a regular guest in Vanda's home, reinforcing Ricardo's presence in absentia and subtly egging on her disdain of Firmino.

As the film opens, Vanda receives a number of friends to commemorate the transferal of Ricardo's remains to the family tomb she has built in his memory. They include two couples—Noémia (Manuela de Freitas) and Fernando (José Martinho) and Angélica (Bárbara Vieira) and Honório (Duarte de Almeida)[10]—as well as the single Maurício (António Machado). Noémia and Fernando are divorced from each other, but they continue together by choice. As Noémia states, they were disunited until their divorce, which paradoxically united them. Angélica and Honório seem happily married, but Angélica has an on-again, off-again affair with the dedicated womanizer Maurício in which vows of eternal love alternate with threats of infinite indifference. Then there is Firmino, whom Vanda constantly and publicly humiliates. But Firmino is not entirely innocent. Early in the film he pretends to strangle Vanda and then stab her with a letter opener.

Faced with unremitting humiliation at Vanda's hands, Firmino kills himself by jumping out of one of the mansion's windows into the flower bed below. While he is agonizing, the group again joins together. In an ironic burlesque moment, while the guests talk, deliverymen clumsily bring in a casket and set it on the pool table, even though Firmino is still alive, if only barely, in the next room.

Before Firmino's demise, Daniel decides to tell Vanda the truth

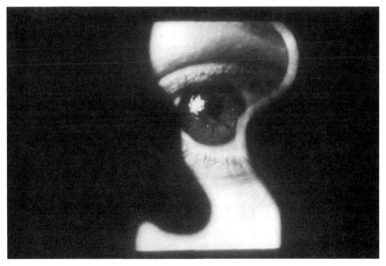

O Passado e o Presente (Cinemateca Portuguesa).

about the automobile accident: he is really her husband Ricardo. Daniel was the one who died in the accident, and he had assumed his twin brother's identity. As he reveals that he—her first husband—is alive, the guests enter the room to inform her that her second husband has died. Given Vanda's pattern of behavior, it does not take long for the deceased Firmino to become her object of devotion, and Ricardo her object of scorn, as if the two men simply trade places in a morbid love triangle. Vanda has replaced the photographs of Ricardo with a large portrait of Firmino, before which she disrobes, as if to offer herself in a way she never did when he was alive. Firmino receives in death what he was unable to attain in life, while Ricardo loses in life what he had when Vanda thought he was dead.

While awaiting Firmino's death, Maurício argues and breaks off with Angélica, then ends his friendship with her husband Honório, who is perhaps the only character who actually believes in marriage. Maurício subsequently makes a move on Noémia, who rejects him based on her love for her ex-husband and current mate, Fernando. Thus, in addition to Vanda's pathological relationships, Oliveira counterposes the faithful but unmarried Noémia and the unfaithful, married Angélica, unmasking what João César Monteiro has referred to as the "contractual monstrosity of the monogamist marriage" (41).

Oliveira's use of music and imagery reinforces this unmasking. Mendelssohn's "Wedding March" plays at key moments, always ironically: after Firmino's feigned gestures of violence against Vanda, when Firmino commits suicide, when his death is announced, after Vanda and Ricardo argue (Torres, *Cinema* 73). While Firmino is agonizing, the gardener finds a dead rat in the flower bed where he had fallen. After we learn of Ricardo's exchange of identities with Daniel, we see an image of a bee on a white rose (also accompanied by the "Wedding March"). Perhaps appropriately, the film's final sequence takes place at a wedding in a nearby church, a scene that is not in Sanches's play. Vanda and Ricardo arrive as the priest says, "Let no one tear asunder that which God unites." As the "Wedding March" plays, they are unable to find a place to sit and are left walking back and forth in the central aisle. Oliveira's satirical view of the institution of bourgeois marriage thus comes to a fitting close.

O Passado e o Presente marks the beginning of Oliveira's systematic exploration of the relationship between theater and the cinema, although his approach is far from that employed in subsequent films. The film is relatively true to the play's dialogues and narrative core, but this is not simply a case of filmed theater, nor does Oliveira assume an explicit "theatricality" as he does in later films. Indeed, he makes a concerted effort to make it more "cinematic," a notion he would render problematic starting with his next film. The three acts of Sanches's play all take place in the living room of Vanda's mansion, although they are separated in time (the second act takes places six months after the first, the third two years after the second). Oliveira's camera is not limited to a single room, and he adds external shots, sequences that are merely referred to in the play (for example, the automobile accident, the group in the cemetery for the transferal of Ricardo's body, judicial proceedings), plus an ending—the church wedding—that differs entirely from the original.

Nevertheless, the film is shot largely inside the walls of a luxurious mansion. This in itself presented a number of challenges for the creation of a dynamic dramatic space. Constant travelings expand the internal space of the action to the point that the camera itself almost becomes a participant observer. It creates a voyeuristic structure by peering through curtains, down hallways, and even through keyholes, as the maid is wont to do. The servants—the maid, the gardener, and the chauffeur—are silent witnesses to the perverse dramas being acted out. But they are not the only voyeurs at play. In the final analysis, we spectators are also voyeurs, peering into a world that attracts and repulses us.

Benilde ou a Virgem-Mãe

For his next feature, Oliveira turned to *Benilde ou a Virgem-Mãe*, a 1947 play by José Régio (1901–69), a friend he had known since the days of "Douro, Faina Fluvial." This was not the first time Oliveira contemplated bringing Régio's work to the screen. In the early 1960s he and Régio collaborated in writing screenplays for two sequences based on Régio's novelistic cycle *A Velha Casa* (The old house; 1945–66), but the Fundo de Cinema declined to fund the project. In 1972 he wrote a screenplay titled "O Caminho" (The road) inspired by diverse facets of Régio's work.[11] It was Régio who brought Sanches's *O Passado e o Presente* to Oliveira's attention, and the short documentary "As Pinturas do Meu Irmão Júlio" deals with Régio's brother. Régio served as a consultant to

O Acto da Primavera. Oliveira would later dedicate *Le Soulier de satin* (1985) to Régio's memory and would again use his work for *A Divina Comédia* (1991), *Mon Cas* (My case; 1986), and *O Quinto Império: Ontem como Hoje* (2004).

Benilde ou a Virgem-Mãe represents a substantial aesthetic shift in Oliveira's exploration of the relations between theater and the cinema, indeed, a shift in his very conception of the cinema, for it is in this film that he begins to establish his characteristic cinematic style. As Oliveira himself once put it, it was with *Benilde* that he freed himself from preconceived notions of the "cinematic," such as the use of camera movement for the sake of camera movement (Baecque and Parsi 179). This shift came about through consideration of the seemingly simple questions, "What is the real difference between theater and cinema? Where does one start and the other end?" (Baecque and Parsi 52).

An incomplete and excessively simple statement of his conclusion is that the theater is not merely that which is presented on stage; it includes everything that constitutes the pro-filmic reality, that is, everything that is placed before the camera prior to a take, since it too is staged. "The theater," Oliveira says, "is living material; it is physical, it is present. The cinema is the phantasm of this material, of the physical reality, but it is more real than the reality itself, in the sense that reality is ephemeral, it constantly escapes us, whereas the cinema, although impalpable and immaterial, can capture it for a certain amount of time, since forever is impossible" (Baecque and Parsi 81). On stage or before a camera, the theater lasts only as long as the performance itself. However, the cinema can preserve at least an image—a "phantasm," to use Oliveira's word—of that performance. Once on film, the theatrical by definition becomes cinematic.

Another question might be added: How does one raise these questions within the formal structure of a film? Oliveira begins to answer this question in *Benilde ou a Virgem-Mãe,* which opens with a rapid, sinuous traveling shot backstage in Lisbon's Tobis Studios, before the camera enters the constructed set per se. Oliveira thus foregrounds an element that is considered quintessentially cinematic—camera movement—while at the same time calling attention to the process of cinematic production before arriving at the space where the drama unfolds. The camera, therefore the cinema, invades and in a sense becomes the theater, or, as João Bénard da Costa puts it, the film travels from the cinema to the theater ("Benilde"). The camera enters the set and focuses on what appears to be an open window looking out on a rural landscape, but then it becomes apparent that it is not a real but rather a painted landscape. What is at stake here is the nature of cinematic reality. Given the fact that the spectator does not actually see the pro-filmic reality, but rather an imperfect image of that reality, how can one distinguish between the real and the artificial if the artificial possesses as much verisimilitude as the real, if both, as Oliveira might say, are mere phantasms of what was placed before the camera?

To render its "theatrical" nature explicit, Oliveira divides the film into three acts through the use of intertitles, and it follows Régio's dialogue to the letter. Each act is shot within a single room of the same house, thus maintaining the play's unity of space. The camera is relatively static throughout, and framing is often frontal, as characters face the camera and break the fourth wall when delivering their lines. As if to emphasize his fidelity to the spirit of the play, Oliveira uses two actors—Maria Barroso and Augusto Figueiredo—who performed in its initial 1947 staging, albeit in different roles. Unlike his adaptation of *O Passado e o Presente*, with its constant camera movement and use of exteriors, in *Benilde* Oliveira makes no attempt to render Régio's play more "cinematic." Despite the adoption of these openly or presumably theatrical elements, we cannot forget that we are watching a film, not a play. As if to emphasize this fact, at the film's end, the initial journey from cinema to theater is reversed through an astounding upward crane shot that reveals the set surrounded by the soundstage. This self-referentiality breaks down the entirely artificial barrier between "what one assumes the cinema to be and what assumes the theater to be" (Baecque and Parsi 81). After all, does the cinema stop when the camera enters the set per se? Does it begin again at the moment the camera initiates its upward crane shot? Everything is equally "real," equally "artificial," equally "cinematic." In subsequent films, Oliveira would take this ontological exploration to its paroxysm, bringing other elements into play, particularly the use of language, the relationship between character and spectator, and the question of the cinematic adaptation of narrative texts.

As the title indicates, *Benilde ou a Virgem-Mãe* tells a story of possible immaculate conception. Benilde (Maria Amélia Aranda) is an eighteen-year-old woman who lives in relative isolation in Portugal's Alentejo region with her widowed father, Estévão (Varela Silva), and their maid Genoveva (Maria Barroso). As the story opens on a rainy night, a physician, Dr. Fabrício (Jacinto Ramos), arrives at their house, summoned by Genoveva. He finds that the local priest, Father Cristóvão (Augusto Figueiredo), was called before him and has been awaiting his arrival. Genoveva asks Dr. Fabício to examine Benilde, since she has been acting strangely. Genoveva is alarmed about what might be happening to her.

Benilde lives in seclusion, since her father pays little attention to her. She sleepwalks in the garden at night, and at times she returns to the house as if in a trance, with a distant look in her eyes, reminding Genoveva of Benilde's deceased mother, who had apparently gone mad. As Genoveva talks to the doctor and the priest, a strange wailing cry is heard outside. Genoveva explains that it is the village idiot or vagrant who sometimes wanders nearby uttering sounds "that seem to come from hell."

Benilde ou a Virgem-Mãe (Cinemateca Portuguesa).

Dr. Fabrício examines Benilde and reveals that she is pregnant. Benilde sees her pregnancy as an act of divine grace, "a great miracle of God's love," because she has never been with a man. She thanks God for having chosen her, since she feels that she is unworthy of this sign of God's love. Her pregnancy, however, provokes different responses from the drama's diverse personages. Indeed, if *Benilde* deals with the possibility of miracles, or at least the mysterious or enigmatic nature of things that can only be explained through faith, just as importantly it concerns the whole complex web of religious, ethical, and social relations, reactions, and constraints that comes into play when such a situation emerges. Set in an extremely conservative, moralistic, and provincial small-town society, the most difficult reaction is that of acceptance.

In *Benilde,* Oliveira is closer to Dreyer—and particularly the Dreyer of *Ordet* (1955)—than in any other of his films. Both are highly theatrical in terms of staging and the use of spoken language, both develop religious themes that involve the possibility of miracles, both include discussions of faith versus science, on the one hand, and skepticism, on the other hand, and both are ultimately ambiguous in terms of their final meaning, although one might argue that Dreyer comes down more clearly on the side of religious faith than does Oliveira, who seems to relish the ambiguity of the situation.

As a representative of science, Benilde's doctor offers explanations based on hysteria, heredity, and childhood education, while at the same time seeing her "simulation and excessive fantasy" as symptomatic of a form of psychological malady that needs to be treated. The priest, however, can only conclude that "nothing is impossible for God" if he is to remain faithful to his own vows and beliefs. Benilde's aunt, Etelvina (Glória de Matos), does not accept the "divine" explanation, but she cannot convince Benilde to change her story. She even comes to suspect Benilde of having had a relationship with the vagrant after Benilde seemingly becomes entranced when she hears the sounds of his howling outside, and she repeatedly asserts that Benilde's marriage with her son Eduardo is now impossible because of the social stigma involved. Benilde's father is also intolerant, saying that he no longer has a daughter and seeing himself as a victim.

Eduardo (Jorge Rolla) evinces a changing, somewhat confused, perspective. His initial reaction is one of shock and rejection, and he even goes so far as to slap Benilde. But his attitude shifts, and he attempts to take advantage of the moment to embrace and kiss Benilde by force. Now that she is impure, he too wants her impurely. But his stance continues to evolve, and he tells her that he wants to marry her no matter what. In the third act, Eduardo asks Benilde's father for her hand. He assumes responsibility for her pregnancy, saying that he took advantage of her one night when she was sleepwalking. Benilde rejects his offer to marry her, since she believes that she is doing God's will and can marry no man. He later tells her that he is willing to live with her as a brother. Again, Benilde cannot accept. God has told her to prepare her soul, because she will soon be called.

In the course of these discussions, Benilde falls ill. After she is taken off to rest, Eduardo tells the priest that she is going to die, and the priest responds that if she does, it will be according to God's will: "There is no death for those who believe, there is only a passage through this world, and there are beings who are not of this world." Eduardo agrees but says that the "world would be smaller if they did not pass through." The film does not resolve the mystery surrounding Benilde. We do not learn the "truth" about her pregnancy. What is left, according to Manoel de Oliveira, is the characters' anguish about the situation. And this anguish represents "a good theme for reflecting about the [modern] world. We are left with the terrible cruelty of doubt" (Baecque and Parsi 173).

As Oliveira was working on *Benilde,* the winds of political change blew over Portugal with hurricane-like force. In April 1974, midrange army officers, disgruntled with the country's colonial wars in Angola, Mozambique, and Guinea Bissau, with the lack of democracy and economic perspectives at home, and with the abuses of the political police, moved against and overthrew the dictatorship that had been in power since the early 1930s. In the immediate aftermath of the revolution there came a period of political instability, as different factions—ranging from the extreme right to the extreme left—jockeyed for power. The summer of 1975 has been referred to as the Verão Quente, or Hot Summer, not because of the weather but because of the political events that took place at the time. The period of instability ended on 25 November 1975, as a moderate wing of the military took power, leading to the establishment of the multiparty parliamentary democracy that exists today.

Benilde ou a Virgem-Mãe was released on 21 November of that year, when the country's attention was turned toward politics, not the metaphysical and religious questions raised by Oliveira's film. According to João Bénard da Costa, the revolution affected Oliveira in a very direct manner. Sectors of the Left occupied his family's factory, which subsequently went bankrupt, causing Oliveira to lose almost all of his personal assets, including the house where he had resided since 1940. Oliveira apparently refers to these events in his 1982 film, *Visita ou Memórias e Confissões* (Visit, or memories and confessions), which will be screened only after his death (Bénard da Costa, *Histórias* 152).

Not surprisingly, the field of cinematic production was also highly politicized at the time. *Benilde* was accused of having nothing to do with the country's political situation and of being antiquated in theme and form. Nevertheless, the film deals with a society thoroughly permeated by certain moral and social concepts, and it is internally dialectical and dialectical "'in opposition to or in contradiction with our own times'" (Oliveira qtd. in "Manoel de Oliveira"). In fact, the film depicts a set of attitudes that characterize a thoroughly repressive, moralistic society, obviously not unlike that which was fostered by the dictatorship since the late 1920s. The largely implicit social setting might be envisioned as a rural, early twentieth-century Portuguese version of the oppressive society Dreyer depicts more explicitly in *Day of Wrath* (1943). João Bénard da Costa has written that *Benilde* can legitimately be seen as "a parable of the lost country that we were and are, as well as of the impossibility of quickly transforming it" (*Histórias* 153).

Amor de Perdição

After *Benilde*, Oliveira approached similar thematic and formal issues (foiled love and the relationship between two distinct forms of artistic expression) in an adaptation of Camilo Castelo Branco's romantic novel, *Amor de Perdição* (1862).[12] Similar to the tragic tale of *Romeo and Juliet*, *Amor de Perdição* tells the story of the impossible love between Teresa Albuquerque and Simão Botelho, scions of wealthy, feuding families in northern Portugal. Because Teresa refuses to marry her cousin Baltasar, whom her father has chosen for her, she is sent away to a prisonlike convent. Simão kills Baltasar and is sentenced to death, but the sentence is later commuted to exile. Teresa dies after seeing Simão embark for exile from her convent window, and he soon dies at sea.

Played out against a vast mural of the conventions of nineteenth-century Portuguese society, with its rigid codes of honor and comportment, Teresa and Simão become symbols of obdurate *amour fou* that leads not only to their own destruction but drags others along with them. Midway through the narrative, Baltasar and his henchmen ambush Simão in an assassination attempt. Simão escapes, slightly wounded. He is taken in by the blacksmith João da Cruz, whose daughter Mariana nurses him back to health. It soon becomes clear that Mariana has fallen in love with Simão. In a not-too-subtle image, at one point she brings Simão roast chicken for dinner. She holds it waist-high in front of her, its open cavity facing him. Her love is much more corporeal than that of Teresa, but it is equally impossible. The distance of social origin impedes her from expressing or fulfilling that love, except through abnegation and dedication, which she demonstrates while in his employ throughout the rest of the story. At one point she even lives in a prison cell with Simão, and she embarks with him when he leaves Portugal for exile. After his death, she kisses his cold lips—the only kiss exchanged in the film—and after his burial at sea, she throws herself into the ocean after him.

The novel, written while Castelo Branco was in jail and based on events that occurred in his uncle's life, had been adapted twice before, in 1921 by Georges Pallu, a Frenchman living in Portugal, and in 1943 by António Lopes Ribeiro, who had produced Oliveira's *Aniki-Bóbó.* Both previous adaptations are rather conventional, perfectly attuned with the aesthetic and ideological timeframes of their production. Despite these earlier adaptations, Oliveira's friend José Régio challenged him to take on Castelo Branco's novel, and he began to think about doing so while he was making *O Passado e o Presente.* The director has said that he initially thought about approaching the novel in much the way he approached Vicente Sanches's play, but viewing Jean-Marie Straub and Danièle Huillet's *Chronicle of Anna Magdalena Bach* (1968), with its focus on music rather than drama, led him to see the novel in a new light (Baecque and Parsi 173).

Oliveira made two slightly different adaptations of the novel, one for television, the other for the cinema. Shot in 16mm and partially financed by Portugal's state television network, Radiotelevisão Portuguesa (RTP), the film was broadcast in six segments in the fall of 1978, preceded by a documentary about the making of the film. As a commentator in the Lisbon newspaper *Expresso* wrote about the introductory documentary at the time, "[T]he idea is to pique the [spectator's] appetite; let's hope that it is not so monotonous that instead of piquing the appetite, it deadens it" (11 November 1978). The series was a disaster. In its weekly listings, that same newspaper suggested that viewers tune in to see how *not* to adapt a novel for the screen. The slow pace, the absence of close-ups, the "theatrical" framing, the acting style, and the use of *tableaux vivants* made *Amor de Perdição* a difficult, if not impossible, sell for the small screen. Beyond the complexity of the film language per se, it was shot in color but broadcast in black and white.

Things changed, however, when the film was released theatrically a year later, leading Oliveira to be recognized as one of the great modern filmmakers. Upon its exhibition in France, *Le Monde* gave it front-page attention. In his review, Louis Marcorelles says that in *Amor de Perdição* Oliveira re-created an epoch and a sensibility in the most surprising and impressive way imaginable and that he reinvented a lost art, "that of the great French, American, and Soviet primitives, for whom the cinema was more than a codified, embalmed art" (Marcorelles 29; Bénard da Costa, "O cinema" 157–58).

The tragic love story told by Castelo Branco in *Amor de Perdição* might seem to lend itself to melodrama, with great appeals to spectator emotion. Oliveira opted for another approach based on continued development of his own concept of cinematic language. Whereas in *Benilde,* Oliveira sought to explore presumed limits between the cinema and the theater, in *Amor de Perdição* he questions the relationship between film and the novel, which is particularly pertinent when dealing with a widely read classic of the nation's literature. In his extensive interview with Antoine de Baecque and Jacques Parsi, Oliveira outlines the dilemma he faced, as well as the solution he found. He recognizes that "in a novel where a lot happens, it would be a waste of time to show everything. Besides, the literary narration, the way of telling the story, the style, the sonorousness of the phrase, [and] the composition are all just as beautiful and interesting as the events that unfold. Therefore, it seemed convenient for me to focus on the text, and that is what I did" (53).

Most adaptations tend to focus on a novel's narrative; they attempt to tell on screen the story the novel tells in written language, using the expressive resources available to the cinema, and they may use some of the novel's language as dialogue or narrative voiceovers. Constraints of the production process, such as time limitations, often lead screenwriters to delete, condense, reduce, or synthesize some episodes or to eliminate or combine some of the work's characters. This is not the path that Manoel de Oliveira chose to follow. Rather, he opted for a certain literalness of adaptation. His statement about the desire to focus on Castelo Branco's text, rather than only the story he told, points toward a rethinking of the notion of adaptation. In other words, the text itself, with its own specific artistic language, is just as important as the events that unfold.

But how does one focus on, or valorize, a written text in a film? Oliveira suggests that "it is not possible to establish a cinematic equivalent to a literary text. But there is another possibility: just as one can film a landscape, one can film a text. Film it or film the voice that reads it. If I show a page from a book so that the spectator can read it on the screen, I am making cinema, and if I introduce someone who reads the text, I am also making cinema. Finally, if I use voiceover narration, I am still making cinema, and I am saving time" (Baecque and Parsi 53).

Although texts of different kinds often appear briefly in films, a film that simply shows a text, page after page in its graphic materiality, would not make for a particularly compelling viewing experience. Using a voiceover to relay purely descriptive passages would also make little sense, because an image can show in an instant what a novel may take several paragraphs to describe.[13] But a voiceover using language taken verbatim from the text can be effective in explaining certain elements of the story, in helping the filmic narrative move forward, or in expressing some of the writer's ideas that might not come through in characters' dialogues. In this sense, language takes on much more importance than it might otherwise have. This is an issue to which we will return throughout this study. As Oliveira says, to capture the beauty of Castelo Branco's text, "The word should not just be a complement to the image. It must be autonomous, like the image and the music. And all of this should fit together in perfect accord" (Baecque and Parsi 72).

Amor de Perdição has not one but two narrators, one male, identified in the credits as "O Delator" (The Informer), another female, named "A Providência" (The Voice of Providence). The narrators represent two aspects of the novel's narrative voice. The Informer serves as an

Amor de Perdição (Cinemateca Portuguesa).

"objective" narrator, providing information about the events that unfold, while the Voice of Providence tends to provide a more subjective or inner perspective. To give but one example, the film opens, during the credits, with an expressionistic, low-angle shot of a jail cell; shadows of bars are reflected on the ceiling. As the credits end, the cell door slowly closes. The next shot is of an official document—a replica of the document that opens Castelo Branco's novel—describing Simão Botelho, who was imprisoned from 1803 to 1805. The Informer reads the document as the spectators see it on screen. But he is interrupted by the Voice of Providence, who speaks in lyrical terms of the tragedy of a person imprisoned and exiled at the age of eighteen, a text that follows the replication of the official document in Castelo Branco's novel. The Informer then breaks back in and finishes by saying, as does the novel, that Simão "had left for India on 17 March 1807." Here, the words of the Informer are purely documentary; those of Providence constitute a sort of subjective metacommentary, even though they too come directly from the text.[14]

Such narrative interventions and alternations occur throughout the film. At times the narration is redundant vis-à-vis the image (it tells us precisely what we see); at others, it is asynchronous, leading or trailing the image or providing information that seemingly has little or nothing to do with the image. At times the voiceover even takes up and continues a character's words. At others the narration assumes an ironic relationship to the image. In addition, characters sometimes think aloud, particularly when they are writing or reading letters (which they often do), but always using texts drawn verbatim from Castelo Branco's novel. To a large extent, the story is told, not shown, as Oliveira opted to dedramatize the source text.

Amor de Perdição comes as close to being a "literal" adaptation as one can imagine. In addition to extensive voiceovers, in respect for Camilo Castelo Branco's narrative Oliveira includes practically all of the novel's key episodes, limiting the kind of narrative condensation that normally takes place in the process of adaptation. It even includes an incident related in a footnote to the first chapter in which an uncle of the author becomes involved in a sword fight. One result of this is the stretching of the film's duration to four hours and twenty-two minutes.

Luis de Pina has suggested that Oliveira gives us "a Camilo [Castelo Branco] proposed not in romantic exasperation facilitated by the classic language of cinema, but rather a permanent distanciation of *visual reading*, of total fidelity to the letter of the novel, and for this very reason it is experimental, new, modern" (198). This distanciation is reinforced by Oliveira's choice to avoid close-ups in order to lessen identification as well as by the film's stylized acting, which inhibits the spectator's involvement with the characters. As Pina puts it, "[T]he actors don't interpret, they simply deliver the text" (198). Their intonation is normally devoid of emotion, and they often face the camera as they speak. This strategy has the effect of drawing spectator attention to the language spoken, and thus to Castelo Branco's text, as well as to the often painterly and hieratic composition of the frame, rather than to what might conventionally be called cinematic "action." Indeed, the film has been termed "an epic without epic action" (Stein).

Amor de Perdição also offers a romantic tale without romanticism. Its overarching concern with novelistic and cinematic conventions—its attempt to adapt the cinema to a literary text rather than the text to the cinema, its overt theatricality, the tension it develops between language and image, character and actor, and screen and spectator, and its distanced gaze—shifts its focus from the obviously emotional issues at stake and the potentially melodramatic nature of the story to questions of form in the modernist tradition from which Oliveira emerged. In his next film, he takes his concern with form and representation a step further.

Francisca

After adapting Camilo Castelo Branco's most famous novel for the screen, Oliveira had hoped to make a film titled "O Negro e o Preto" (The black and the black) in collaboration with playwright Vicente Sanches. The film was to deal with the absence of love in apparently loving relationships in a sort of parable of the modern world (Clarens 68). When that project did not work out, he turned to a recently published novel in which Castelo Branco is a major character—Agustina Bessa-Luís's *Fanny Owen* (1979)—with a film titled *Francisca*. Oliveira has explained that he was already familiar with the story of Francisca (Fanny) Owen, and he felt that he could film it quickly with the crew he had already contracted for "O Negro e o Preto." He wrote the screenplay in a week (Baecque and Parsi 71).

Francisca was the first of numerous collaborations with Bessa-Luís, who is one of the major figures of contemporary Portuguese literature. Oliveira would later turn to her work for his films *Abraham's Valley* (1993), *The Convent* (1995), *Party* (1996), *Inquietude* (1998), *O Princípio da Incerteza* (The uncertainty principle; 2002), and *Espelho Mágico* (2005). The writer also appears in Oliveira's autobiographical *Porto da Minha Infância* (2001). *Francisca* was also Oliveira's first collaboration with producer Paulo Branco, whom he sought out after the success of *Amor de Perdição* in Paris, where Branco programmed the Action-République movie theater. Branco produces with Gemini Films in Paris and Madragoa Filmes in Lisbon and has worked with such directors as Alain Tanner, Wim Wenders, Raoul Ruiz, Danièle Dubroux, and Werner Schroeter. He is also an important distributor and exhibitor in Portugal, and he produced all of Manoel de Oliveira's films from *Francisca* to *O Quinto Império*.

Like *Amor de Perdição, Fanny Owen/Francisca* is based on a true story, the tragic love affair between José Augusto Pinto de Magalhães, who was a friend of Castelo Branco, and Fanny Owen, the daughter of a British colonel, Hugh Owen (1784–1860), and a Brazilian, Maria Rocha Owen. Oliveira's adaptation of the novel is not quite as "literal" as that of *Amor de Perdição,* and his narrative strategy is also different. Here he makes extensive use of intertitles rather than a voiceover narration, except in the initial sequence. At times the intertitles simply place the action in a given locale (for example, "Camilo's room in the Paris Hotel, in Porto") or at a given time ("A few days later . . ."). Other intertitles synthesize the characters' actions or feelings and provide contextualization ("It was a masked ball, in Porto, and José Augusto had gone to amuse himself, but he soon regretted having done so; his mourning for his mother was too recent . . ."). At the outset an intertitle situates the film in historical terms, although the historical events referred to have little to do, at least directly, with the drama that unfolds. The narrative blocs delineated by intertitles, generally comprising one or more sequence shots, represent brief moments of the story being related. Driving the action are the characters' dialogues, which are normally taken directly from the novel, although Oliveira constructed some from descriptive passages. One critic has written that "Manoel de Oliveira's entire effort . . . consisted in staging the dialogues" (Tesson 13). Although that statement may be somewhat hyperbolic, it points toward the continued centrality of language and the diminished role of action in Oliveira's work.

Francisca opens with a woman reading a letter beside a window covered by a translucent white curtain. The female sender's voiceover reads the letter that the woman is reading. It is a letter of condolences. As she finishes reading, the camera slowly moves in until it frames only the curtain, while the voiceover repeats the letter, which was written by Maria Rocha Owen and dated 23 September 1854. The camera remains focused on the curtain, on which are superimposed the credits and the initial intertitles. The letter expresses condolences for the loss of the recipient's brother, whom she considered a son. At this point, however, the spectator does not know who the sender and recipient are—except for the name of the sender—nor the specific events the letter evokes. It points, however, to tragic events that will be the focus of the film, which thus unfolds as a long flashback.

Maria Rocha Owen was Fanny Owen's mother. Fanny died on 3 August 1854, less than two months before the date of the letter. The other death in question is that of José Augusto, the brother of Dona Josefa Borges, the woman who appears in the initial sequence, and the son-in-law of Maria Rocha Owen. *Francisca* deals with the events leading up to their deaths, but just as the camera cannot see the external reality on the other side of the window because of the curtain, the truth of the events the film evokes may ultimately be just as inaccessible. As if to reinforce the elusiveness of truth, at the end of the film Camilo Castelo Branco (henceforth, Camilo) and two of his friends, seated in a bar, offer several possible causes for José Augusto's death—suicide, murder, illness, opium—but then decide that the best solution is to have another glass of conhaque.

José Augusto is a twenty-plus-year-old *morgado*, a term used to designate the oldest son and heir to a family's fortune. He is wealthy and idle. He has literary airs but is intellectually mediocre. His life revolves around evenings at the theater, often in the company of a married woman, discussions in local cafés, and efforts to pursue amorous relationships. He is at once haughty, inconstant, and insecure. Camilo,

Teresa Meneses as Francisca (Cinemateca Portuguesa).

a young writer of somewhat lesser social standing who is known for his acerbic pen, met José Augusto when they were students together in Coimbra. He later befriends him but often refers to him as pernicious, thus assuming a duplicitous position.

The initial post-credits sequence introduces José Augusto at a masked ball not long after his mother's death. Facing the camera dressed in a red cape with his black mask hanging loosely on his chest, he seems rather sinister or diabolical. As the masked revelers dance around him, the atmosphere is simultaneously spirited, fantastic, and infernal. José Augusto turns and walks off while the dancing continues, clearly a misfit amidst the revelry. The film then cuts to Camilo's hotel room and a conversation between José Augusto and Camilo about love, women, and happiness. José Augusto meets Fanny Owen and her sister Maria at another masked ball. He is first interested in Maria, and he begins to frequent their house. But when he suspects that Camilo is attracted to Fanny, he expresses his love for her, telling Camilo that he will kill anyone who loves her. He later tells Camilo that he plans to flee with Fanny, and Camilo tries to warn Fanny not to go with him. She responds that he is an envious and evil man and that she now understands why honest people dislike him.

Fanny flees with José Augusto. He takes her to his house in Lodeiro, but he soon leaves for Porto, where he again goes out with Raquel, a wealthy married woman he has been seeing. Fanny, in the meantime, is a virtual prisoner, with only the maid and an occasional visitor as company. While José Augusto is in Porto, Camilo delivers to him several letters that Fanny has apparently written to another man. José Augusto says that he no longer loves Fanny, but he marries her anyway. He will not consummate the marriage, however, as a matter of "honor." She remains cloistered, imprisoned by the institution of marriage and social conventions. Fanny is unable to convince José Augusto of her innocence—her virginity—and when she discovers a letter from her sister Maria and insists on seeing it, José Augusto slaps her. Their relationship ends in tragedy. Fanny becomes ill and dies of tuberculosis, although in reality she had died long before, sacrificed and humiliated by her husband's obsessions, which do not end with her death. He orders an autopsy to confirm his suspicions. An intertitle informs us that Camilo has asked the doctor to verify her virginity.

After the autopsy, José Augusto keeps Fanny's heart in alcohol in a glass vial in the chapel in Lodeiro. In one of the film's eeriest scenes, one day he is in the chapel as a maid comes in to clean up. He begins talking to himself about the heart, "a still muscle, like a broken clock. It wasn't impressive when you could feel it beating in her chest, in her pulse. . . . Amazing things came out of it: the fate of a man, and even more. The absolute and vindictive truth was also produced there." The vial drops on the floor, and he picks up her heart and holds it in his hand, while the maid flees in fear. Oliveira films the scene in the darkened chapel with the camera focused on José Augusto. He then repeats from José Augusto's perspective, focusing on the maid's reaction. When asked about the taboo of showing the heart, Oliveira responded, "But it's historical! It really exists." Apparently Fanny's heart was preserved in formaldehyde in the hospital where the autopsy was performed (Baecque and Parsi 61).

In *Francisca*, Oliveira offers a morbid conclusion to his tetralogy of frustrated love. As in *Amor de Perdição*, its mise-en-scène is exquisite, capturing in detail the spaces where the drama unfolds. Oliveira's hieratic positioning of actors, frequently posed in such a way that even in dialogues they address the camera, not the person to whom they are talking in the diegesis, gives them a sense of being somehow disembodied, spectral visions in some sort of preordained tragic dance. In some sequences the music reinforces this ethereal presence, particularly in external nighttime scenes in which "fantastic sounds mix with liturgic chants in such a way as to ritualize tenebrous actions" (Paes 95). In this film Oliveira takes the experiments with cinematic discourse that began with *Benilde* about as far as they can go without become overtly theatrical, which is what occurs in his next film.

To the Limit

After completing the tetralogy, Manoel de Oliveira took on one of the most ambitious projects of his career: the filming of Paul Claudel's epic Catholic drama, *Le Soulier de satin* (The satin slipper; 1929), a play so extensive that it is rarely staged in its entirety. Oliveira had hoped to film the whole play, but that would have resulted in at least an eleven-hour film. He was therefore compelled to edit Claudel's text down to a more manageable six hours and forty minutes. He did, however, maintain the play's structure, including at least the most significant portion of each of its fifty-two scenes, while at the same time adding four additional scenes of his own.

Le Soulier de satin (1985) is a key work in Oliveira's filmography for a number of reasons. First, it offers continuity to the concerns about unfulfilled love that animate his previous four films. Second, it establishes a bridge to subsequent films such as *Non ou a Vã Glória de Mandar* (No or the vain glory of command; 1990), *Um Filme Falado* (A talking picture; 2003), and *O Quinto Império* (2004), bringing a concern with history and empire to the fore. Third, it represents the culmination of Oliveira's exploration of the relationship between film and theater. And fourth, it was his first film shot entirely in French.[15]

The setting of *Le Soulier de satin* is "the world" in the late sixteenth or early seventeenth century, with scenes set in Lisbon, Prague, Cádiz, Mogador, Sicily, various places in the Americas, and a ship in the mid-Atlantic. The drama takes place in the period after Portuguese King Sebastian (1554–78) disappeared and was presumably killed leading a disastrously ill-conceived crusade in northern Africa in an attempt to expand the Portuguese empire and the Catholic faith. The disappearance of King Sebastian led to Portugal's humiliation and domination by Spain and marked the end of the period of national grandeur characterized by the voyages of discovery. The king's disappearance—his body was never found—also generated one of the most important myths of Portuguese history, the idea that Sebastian would one day return, emerging from the mist to reconstitute Portugal's rightful place in the world. More abstractly and more durably, the messianic myth has to do with the hope of national regeneration. Oliveira refers to King Sebastian's debacle in each of the later films mentioned above, and he is the central focus of *O Quinto Império*. Through a series of intertitles after the introductory sequence as well as two of the scenes that he added to the play, Oliveira explicitly anchors *Le Soulier de satin* in the wake of a failed European imperial thrust against the Islamic world in a way that Claudel does not. Indeed, this more precise critical contextualization tempers the undeniably imperialist tenor of Claudel's play.

Within this broad context, *Le Soulier de satin* tells the story of Don Rodrigue (Luís Miguel Cintra) and Doña Prouhèze (Patricia Barzyk), who, like the characters in Oliveira's tetralogy, are never able to consummate their love. When they meet, Prouhèze is wed through an arranged marriage to an older nobleman, Don Pélage (Franck Oger), for whom she feels respect but not love. Nevertheless, before she leaves on a journey, Prouhèze swears that she will never dishonor her husband, even though that means not fulfilling her love for Rodrigue. She offers a satin slipper to a statue of the Virgin Mary—thus the play's title—so that when she rushes "on evil it may be with limping foot."

The king of Spain chooses Rodrigue to represent him in the conquest of the Americas, but Rodrigue does not depart immediately. Knowing of Prouhèze's love for Rodrigue, Pélage insists that she go to Mogador in North Africa, a Spanish outpost under the command of Don Camille (Jean-Pierre Bernard), whom Pélage does not trust and who has previously attempted to gain Prouhèze's favor. She is to replace Camille and make him her lieutenant in Spain's struggle to fend off the Moors' military advances. The king, however, soon has misgivings about sending Prouhèze to command "a castle half-abandoned between sand and sea, between treason and Islam." He decides to send Rodrigue, who is ready to depart for the Americas, to Mogador to give Prouhèze a letter suggesting that she return to Spain. Rodrigue thus sails to Mogador, where he is met by Camille. Although he longs to do so, he does not see Prouhèze. Rather, Camille delivers a note from her saying, "I stay, you go." After a tense dialogue, Rodrigue leaves the outpost without seeing his beloved. He soon departs on his mission to the Americas, where he becomes Viceroy of the Indies.

Ten years go by. Pélage dies, and Prouhèze marries Camille, who had converted to Islam, as the only way to continue her mission at Mogador and constrain the renegade's misdeeds. He held Prouhèze a virtual prisoner, occasionally whipping or torturing her. Separated by the forces of history and duty, as well as the Atlantic Ocean, Prouhèze and Rodrigue meet again only once, on a ship off the coast of Mogador, after Rodrigue receives a letter from Prouhèze that has taken a decade to reach him. In their meeting, Prouhèze delivers her daughter Sept-Épées (Anne Cosigny) to him. Camille has demanded Rodrigue's withdrawal from Mogador in exchange for Prouhèze's freedom, but neither of the lovers will place their own happiness above honor and duty. Their love—like that of Simão and Teresa in *Amor de Perdição* and José Augusto and Fanny in *Francisca*—will not be consummated on this earth. By the drama's end, which takes another ten years, Rodrigue, who has been sent in disgrace to the Philippines because he abandoned his post in the Americas to sail to Mogador, is forced to sell paintings of saints to poor fishermen to survive and is eventually sold as a slave to two elderly nuns.

Like his source text, Oliveira's *Le Soulier de satin* self-reflexively melds high drama, comedy, farce, philosophical speculation, allegory, fantasy, and politics on a grand scale into a tale of the denial of self for a larger purpose. This theme may not necessarily resonate with modern audiences, especially when packaged in a film with a duration of almost seven hours and a cinematic discourse that is so distant from mainstream film conventions, a discourse that is at once primitive, remitting to the origins of the cinema, and ultramodern in its self-reflexivity and its aesthetic daring.

Le Soulier de satin is Oliveira's most hieratic work, both in terms of the mise-en-scène and the actors' mode of representation. He films the scenes of Claudel's play in *tableaux vivants*, generally using sequence

Anne Cosigny (standing) in *Le Soulier de satin*
(Cinemateca Portuguesa).

shots. After the initial sequence, which I will describe below, the film explicitly assumes a high level of theatricality. The sets and backdrops are often painted, the props are obviously fake, the waves at sea seem like revolving rolls of papier-mâché, leaping whales are made of painted cardboard, and so forth. Much of the drama is set outdoors, yet the film does not include a single external shot. With the exception of the two sermons near the beginning that evoke the humiliation of Portugal's domination by Spain, it was shot entirely in Lisbon's Tobis Studios. Actors generally face a static camera when delivering their lines, with no pretense of a fourth wall. Rather than attempt to make Claudel's play more cinematic, as he did in his adaptation of Vicente Sanches's *O Passado e o Presente*, Oliveira continued the mode of representation developed in *Amor de Perdição* and *Francisca*. He took his cues in the composition of *Le Soulier de satin* from the play itself.

Oliveira was drawn to *Le Soulier de satin* less because of its ultimate religious meaning than by the aesthetic possibilities it afforded. More specifically, he was drawn to the beauty and musicality of Claudel's language. In fact, he has said that for him *Le Soulier de satin* is an opera because of the musicality inherent in the mixture of voices and the poetic flow of words (Torres, *Cinema*). One of the reasons that he sought to make the film as static as possible was to compel spectators to use their ears as much as their eyes, and this is no doubt the meaning of the film's final word: "écoutez."

But *Le Soulier de satin* also gave Oliveira the opportunity to take his reflections on the relationship between film and theater to their paroxysm. As he has put it, the film is "the logical and no doubt conflictive conclusion to a moment of my work on the difference between what one presumes the cinema to be and what one presumes the theater to be, or between literature and what is presumed to be real life. Between what one supposes to be the different modes of representation, between the use of more artificial or more natural sets, or that hidden alliance between image and music, or between a supposed historical vision and a supposedly imaginary or imagined vision" (Baecque and Parsi 81–82). Oliveira would later recognize that with *Le Soulier de satin* he was pushing these reflections to a limit beyond which it would be impossible to go.

The opening sequence of *Le Soulier de satin* represents the perfect illustration of the view of the relationship between film and theater that

Manoel de Oliveira had been developing since *Benilde.* The sequence opens in a theater lobby, with the camera looking toward closed glass doors and several ushers positioned beside them. Outside, a crowd waits noisily to enter. The theater manager appears, walks toward the camera, and announces the play that is about to begin: "The Satin Slipper or The Worst Is Not the Surest. Spanish play in Four Days by Paul Claudel" (Claudel xxiv). He twice turns to walk away, then returns and continues his brief introduction. As he finishes, he raises one arm, and we hear a flourish from a single trumpet; he raises the other, and we hear a flourish of several horns.[16]

The manager then motions for the ushers to open the doors, and the audience starts to file in, while the dissonance of the orchestra warming up fills the soundtrack. The camera backs into the auditorium as the spectators enter and begin to take their seats. From near the front of the room, it tilts up to reveal the fully dressed cast standing on the first balcony. An actor leaves the group and goes down to the auditorium. The camera tilts back down to the auditorium doors, where the actor—the play's Announcer—soon appears, and it pans to accompany him as he walks around to the audience's right until he reaches and goes up on the stage. He taps his cane several times and the curtain opens, revealing not a theatrical set, as one might expect, but rather a movie screen positioned stage right. The Announcer begins to establish the context for the drama to follow, saying, "Let us fix our gaze, I pray you, brethren, on that point of the Atlantic Ocean some degrees below the Line, equidistant from the Old World and the New" (Claudel 1). Up to this point we are dealing with an impressive single take that backs into the auditorium from the theater lobby, tilts up to the cast on the balcony, then back down and around the hall to accompany the Announcer onto the stage, and finally records the beginning of his introduction.

The first cut places the camera at the rear of the auditorium focusing on the stage, and more specifically on the movie screen on stage. It slowly travels in until the object on the screen—a small ship floating on the open sea (or better, a miniature ship on an artificial sea)—becomes visible as the Announcer continues his introduction: "There is perfectly well shown here the wreck of a dismasted ship, drifting at the mercy of the waves." The camera's forward movement continues until the screen positioned on stage fills the screen that we as spectators are watching, or, to put it differently, until the stage becomes the screen. We then see a Jesuit priest (Luís Miguel Cintra) tied to the main-mast as the ship rocks back and forth. He thanks God for his predicament and prays for his brother Rodrigue.

The next cut is not to another angle of the priest, nor to another scene of Claudel's play, but rather to a film projector in the rear of the theater auditorium, the projector that is exhibiting the images of the Jesuit priest that we have been watching. The camera, facing toward the projector and away from the stage, then travels back, revealing audience members looking up in fascination at the screen above, illuminated by the flickering light of the projection.

Again, Oliveira foregrounds ontological questions about the relationship between the theater and the cinema. At the outset, we are presented with images of a theatrical setting in its physical reality—the building, with its lobby, auditorium, audience, and stage. And yet, as the film assumes a certain theatricality, that is, when the Announcer goes on stage and begins his introductions, *Le Soulier de satin* becomes explicitly cinematic, although it is announced as a play and is attributed to Paul Claudel.

The film's ending reinforces Oliveira's self-reflexive view of the relationship between theater and cinema. After the final scene of Claudel's play, the camera dollies back to reveal the film crew working at the foot of the stage, not in the auditorium where the film began but rather in Lisbon's Tobis Studios where it was shot. In other words, *Le Soulier de satin* begins in the theater and ends in the cinema. The camera then tilts up to a platform above the stage, where there stands a chorus in modern dress. As the film ends, the chorus repeats over and over the word "écoutez" (listen), again emphasizing the importance of the spoken word to both the theater and the cinema. In many ways, the film's movement is the movement of language, not that of the camera, which is often static once the drama per se gets under way.

The actors' mode of representation, which Oliveira had been developing since *Benilde ou a Virgem-Mãe*, contributes to directing focus toward language. Characters generally look in the direction of—or at—the camera as they deliver their lines in a dispassionate manner, rather than at the person to whom they are speaking in the diegesis.[17] Such a gaze has long been considered taboo in mainstream cinema, since it tends to break down the scene's desired "realism," although it has frequently been used as a distancing effect in independent or avant-garde works (such as Godard's *La Chinoise* [1967] and *Weekend* [1968]). Responding to a question about his strategy, Oliveira has said that "this taboo presupposes that there is a hidden spectator, because if he is present, it will disrupt the action. My perspective is precisely to put the spectator in the action. In this way, the spectator goes from a passive, manipulated attitude to an active attitude in which he should draw his own conclusions and undertake a criticism of what he sees" (Baecque and Parsi 127). Oliveira suggests that through their narrative and visual construction, many films tell the spectator what to think (who is good and bad, for example), thus underestimating his or her intelligence and capacity for analysis. And this, Oliveira continues, makes for bad spectators who get into the habit of not thinking when they see a film.

Le Soulier de satin combines a straightforward "theatrical" representation involving the major and secondary characters with a number of phantasmagoric sequences that often serve as a kind of metacommentary on their drama. In a scene that takes place along the pilgrimage route to Santiago, for example, Saint James, as the constellation Orion, offers a soliloquy on the distance that separates Africa from America and Prouhèze from Rodrigue. Following Rodrigue's first visit to Mogador, where Prouhèze refuses to see him, is a scene of a double shadow of a man and woman. They sit, back to back, behind a sheet on stage, with only their silhouettes visible, as they recite in tandem—and in an incantatory tone—their lines about their severed being and their desire for unity.

After the double shadow comes one of the most remarkable scenes in the film, the one that most directly remits to silent cinema, and more specifically to Georges Méliès's *Le Voyage dans la lune* (1902). The actress Marie-Christine Barrault speaks the moon's extensive soliloquy through a hole cut in the black backdrop, her face the face in the moon. According to Oliveira, the scene was very challenging to shoot, because the soliloquy is quite long and it had to be done in a single take, with the actress restraining her emotion to allow the spectator to feel the emotion contained in Claudel's words (Baecque and Parsi 120).

Because of its length and complexity, *Le Soulier de satin* was never released commercially in Portugal. For it and the whole of his work to this point, Oliveira received a Golden Lion at the 1985 Venice Film

Festival as well as the L'Âge d'Or Prize from the Brussels Cinemathèque. The film also represented the first time Oliveira worked with Luís Miguel Cintra, who would become one of the director's regulars.

Mon Cas

With *Mon Cas* (My case; 1988), Oliveira's work takes yet another turn, without abandoning his abiding concern for the theater. The core of *Mon Cas* is José Régio's farcical one-act play, *O Meu Caso* (1957). Its setting is a theater stage, although the play that is presumably to take place never actually does. But the film is far from being a simple adaptation of Régio's play. Rather, it stages the play almost as written before transforming it into something altogether different. Oliveira does not limit himself to Régio's play. *Mon Cas* also incorporates a portion of one of Samuel Beckett's "Fizzles" and of the Book of Job.

Mon Cas is perhaps the most daring of Oliveira's films, and it is the one that deals most directly with the relationship between art and life, a subject he would take up again in *I'm Going Home* (2001). But it also deals with questions such as the possibility of narration—a question that runs throughout his work—as well as the relationship between the human, the divine, and redemption in a world in dissolution. Pedro Borges has referred to *Mon Cas* as Oliveira's most religious film (*Régio* 37).

The film begins similarly to *Le Soulier de satin*, by self-reflexively calling attention to itself qua film. After the credits, a female voiceover says, in French, "He loves me, he loves me not." As the lights come up, the first image is of a movie camera. Oliveira's crew enters an empty theater and sets up its equipment in front of the stage. Unlike *Le Soulier*, however, there are no spectators other than the crew. When the crew is ready, Oliveira gets the filming process under way with the traditional "lights, camera, action!" and then one of the crew members holds up a clapboard: "Mon Cas—First Repetition." The word "répétition" in French, by the way, can mean either "repetition" or "rehearsal," an ambiguity that fits well with the director's purpose in the film.

When the play is about to begin, an unknown man or Desconhecido invades the stage in a greatly agitated state. He complains about the falsity of the theater: fake moustaches, wigs, painted faces, artificial props. Nothing is real, and yet the actors participate in the charade as if it were perfectly natural. According to him, none of it is of any import;

what matters is *his* problem, *his* case, of universal significance, about which he wants to tell the audience.

His disruption of the theatrical space where a play is about to begin has a tumultuous effect on those who participate in it, and their often heated dialogues lay out the frequently selfish interests at stake. The Desconhecido (Luís Miguel Cintra) feels that he has always been marginalized and unfairly silenced, even though he believes that his case has some sort of transcendent meaning. The theater manager (Axel Bougousslavsky), who should have kept the man out, is worried about his job. He has been employed there for twenty years, his wife is a paralytic, his oldest son is out of work, and his two youngest sons are not old enough to hold jobs. Unemployment would be disastrous for him. Nevertheless, the Desconhecido belittles his concerns. The actress (Bulle Ogier), who has arrived late for what she calls the most important role of her life, frets about the incident's impact on her career. The author (Fred Personne) wants the play to go on, saying that it has taken him five years to stage his play and that it must continue, even though he has had to make so many concessions along the way—to producers, critics, actors—that little is left of his original work. A representative of the audience stands up to defend their perspective. All they want is a little diversion from the tedium and toil of everyday life, and yet they are unable to have even that. The author says that they should lower the curtain for the play to begin, and the audience member starts to return to his seat, but another yells for him to remain on stage, since he too has become part of the play. The Desconhecido again tries to tell about his situation, but the curtain falls, interrupting him mid-sentence. On the curtain are representations of the traditional masks of comedy and tragedy. The first version offers Régio's play as it was written, in a farcical, often burlesque style, and in an art-déco set. In this sequence, for the first time since *O Passado e o Presente*, Oliveira gives actors free rein to express their characters' emotions within the play's dramatic context.

Oliveira, however, does not leave it at that. He films the play not once, but three times, each time with a somewhat different staging. In fact, the film's title was originally to have been "Mon Cas—Repetitions." Oliveira has said that the repetitions derived from the idea that life is repetition and that art serves to replicate life. The stagings are different, just as one day may be like the next without being the same

(*Régio* 38–39). The second "take," or repetition, is done in the mode of a silent film: it is in black and white and accelerated motion. There is no dialogue, but a narrative voiceover repeats a passage from Beckett's "I Gave Up before Birth" from *For to End Again and Other Fizzles,* while the actors perform their roles. The shift in color and rhythm establishes an aesthetic link to silent film—which is reinforced by the fact that we hear the sound of a projector—while the voiceover occasions a significant change in mood. Although visually the repetition is much quicker and lighter than the first take, it is also much weightier. Beckett's brief text begins with the following words: "I gave up before death, it is not possible otherwise, but birth there had to be, it was he, I was inside, that's how I see it" (45). Through the juxtaposition of a lighthearted visual representation and Beckett's text, Oliveira raises questions about the conflict between art, the illusion of representation, the human condition, and the impossibility of fulfillment (Fonseca, "Mon Cas" 2).

The third repetition returns to normal motion and to color, but the soundtrack is played backwards, rendering the dialogues entirely unintelligible, which seems highly appropriate for the question of the role of art in a world in dissolution. Midway through this version, a crew member goes onto the stage and sets up a table, on which he mounts a video projector. He then opens the doors at the rear of the stage and pulls down a screen. He returns to the table and puts a tape in the machine. Recalling the documentary images at the end of *Acto da Primavera,* the video projects scenes of war and environmental devastation: tanks, explosions, guns, gas masks, wounded, dead bodies, massacres, executions, Kosovo, pollution, dead animals, fowl covered in oil, starvation. In short, we see a world in a state of utter madness, and violence comes to form the backdrop as the play continues on stage. However, the actors who have formed a silent audience at the back of the stage slowly turn their attention from the play to the images on the screen, signaling that life is of much more import than the now-unintelligible clash of egos taking place on stage. At the end, a print of Picasso's *Guernica*—painted in 1937 to protest the bombing of a Basque village—is lowered in front of the screen, offering a powerful antiwar statement. The curtain falls, and rather than the masks of tragedy and comedy, as occurred with the other repetitions, we see only the mask of tragedy, its mouth agape as in Edvard Munch's *The Scream.*

Luís Miguel Cintra and Bulle Ogier as Job and his wife in *Mon Cas* (Cinemateca Portuguesa).

Following the three repetitions of Régio's *O Meu Caso*, character-ized by a conflict of vanities on stage, increasing unintelligibility, and images of violence and horror, the film shifts to the story—or "case"—of the biblical Job, a poetic story of steadfastness and faith. First, it opens to a modern urban wasteland à la *Blade Runner*, where Job (Luís Miguel Cintra), his faced covered with lesions, sits beside his wife (Bulle Ogier), both of them facing the camera. Oliveira constructed the text of this section from different passages of the Book of Job. The first passage, spoken after his wife tells him that he should "curse God and die," is drawn from chapter 3, where Job curses the day of his birth. After that, his friends Eliphaz, Bildad, Zophar, and Elihu (played by the same actors who represent the theater manager, the author, and the two spectators, respectively) intervene with words of consolation or suggestions of his guilt and need for repentance. As in the Bible, Job responds to each of them in extended dialogues drawn from different chapters of the book. Finally, God responds to Job (chapter 38). Obviously, one cannot film God, so Oliveira objectifies His voice with the use of loudspeakers and marks His presence with bright flashing lights, as if speaking "out of the storm."

At the end of this segment, the film cuts to a scene of Job after God has restored his prosperity. He sits on a throne in a theatrical setting, with painted backdrops, that resembles an ideal city in the style of Piero della Francesca. Beside him is his wife and Da Vinci's *Mona Lisa*. Young women dance around him spreading flower petals on the floor. This harmonious vision, which is the result of Job's faith, is in stark contrast to the urban wasteland of the previous sequence as well as the world in dissolution represented by the earlier documentary images. The camera slowly tracks in to a close-up of the painting. The contrast with Picasso's *Guernica* could not be more striking. The film then cuts to an image of the *Mona Lisa* on a small video monitor. The camera backs off to show Oliveira and his crew filming the set we have just seen in an otherwise empty auditorium. The film ends as the camera moves in on the video monitor until it focuses only on Mona Lisa's mouth.

According to Oliveira, José Régio's *O Meu Caso* offers "both a warning to mankind and an appeal to God, anticipating the hoped-for concord of this disconcerted world where a dissonant humanity, in its long journey, has shown itself incapable of going beyond the theory of 'men of good will.' It is a questionable world, where humans don't understand each other and where God, if He exists, remains silent, dead or off-screen as a spectator" ("'O Meu Caso'" 36). The juxtaposition of modern and time-less perspectives allows for reflection on the difficulty of communication, the vanities that sometimes underlie what may seem to be disinterested activities, human beings' complicity with the horrors of today's world, and the role of art in contemporary society. A religious reading of the film is certainly plausible, particularly in its utopian image of Job in the ideal city, but Oliveira has made it clear that in his view art is not responsible for saving the world; rather, it constitutes a reflection on the world, but without providing solutions or answers. They are up to the spectator.

Os Canibais

Os Canibais (Cannibals; 1988) takes the satirical, Buñuelian aspect of Oliveira's work—first seen in *O Passado e o Presente*—to a paroxysm. The film is based on the homonymous short narrative by the little-known late romantic writer Álvaro de Carvalhal (1844–68), an author of "sinister stories of cruelty, crime, animal realism, excessive and morbid fantasy" (*Régio* 45). Written in a florid but highly ironic and self-reflexive prose, Carvalhal's tale and Oliveira's film deal with the beautiful young Margarida (Leonor Silveira), who falls for the mysterious Viscount of Aveleda (Luís Miguel Cintra) during an elegant ball, rejecting the attention of a suitor, Dom João (Don Juan, played by Diogo Dória), who is consumed with jealousy. Shortly after midnight, Margarida and the Viscount go out into the garden. Dom João furtively accompanies them, watching them unseen. After Margarida declares her affinity with the Viscount, he asks her, "If I were a cold, inert cadaver, animated by some ingenious mechanism, but with a living heart beating in my dead body, could you embrace me without repugnance? Would you rest your forehead on the chest of a corpse?" Despite finding the question somewhat strange, Margarida responds that she would accept, "even if our nuptial bed is in the cemetery." Not a smart response on her part. After they kiss and the Viscount walks away, the jealous Dom João approaches and tells Margarida that he has witnessed her infamy and that he is curious to know if a bullet can open a passageway through a cranium.

Some time later, Margarida and the Viscount marry. On their wedding night, after the guests retire to their rooms, the Viscount reveals his secret to his bride: he is in fact a statue, part human and part machine. Only his heart and head are human. He opens his robe, loosens a buckle, and his mechanical arms and legs drop onto the floor, leaving only his trunk. Horrified, Margarida leaps out of an open window. Unable to reach the poison he has prepared in case his spouse rejected him, the Viscount teeters and rolls off his chair into the fireplace, where he is devoured by flames. Dom João, who has been waiting outside for the appropriate moment to kill the Viscount, enters the room and sees his rival's burning torso.

The next morning, the bride's father awakes and goes downstairs for a late breakfast. When he sees that nothing has been prepared, he decides to go to the Viscount's room. He notices an odd smell, and he sees what he takes to be roast meat in the fireplace. Knowing of the Viscount's eccentricities, he assumes that the meat is some delicacy that the Viscount has prepared as a surprise for them. He and his two sons eat a filling breakfast at their host's expense. As they are finishing, they hear a gunshot and rush outside, where they find Margarida lying dead on the ground. She hit her head when she jumped out of the window. On the ground beside her, with a self-inflicted gunshot wound to the chest, is Dom João. Although in grave condition, he is still able to tell them what has happened, and he indicates that they should look in the fireplace to find the Viscount. Aghast at their unintended cannibalism, the bride's father and his sons see no option other than suicide. That is, until one son, who is a magistrate, remembers that they are the sole heirs to the Viscount's immense fortune since he had no other relatives. In Carvalhal's short story, they praise God, forgetting about suicide. In its final sentence, they "[pounce] upon the magistrate like starving mastiffs upon the tough skin of a Lamego ham."

José Régio first brought Carvalhal's carnivorous tale to Oliveira's attention, and the director took advantage of the opportunity to shoot his first—and thus far only—opera. By doing so, he also satisfied a desire of composer João Paes, who had worked with Oliveira on every film since *O Passado e o Presente* and expressed interest in writing an opera based on a topic of Oliveira's choice (*Régio* 46). Oliveira was attracted to the idea of filming the story as an opera by the idea of having the Viscount sing his final words while lying in the fireplace, his torso consumed by flames. Oliveira wrote the screenplay, as is his habit, using language taken directly from the source text. Paes is credited for the libretto as well as the music, but Oliveira has stressed that the words all come from Carvalhal and that he himself selected the passages to be used and organized them into a screenplay (Baecque and Parsi 92).

The decision to shoot *Os Canibais* as an opera also allowed Oliveira to transform the kind of narrator he had used in *Amor de Perdição* into a character of the film. As in the earlier film, here too one might speak of two "narrators," one who narrates verbally, the other who intervenes musically. According to Oliveira, the violinist Niccolò, whom the director sometimes refers to as Paganini, is somewhat of a demonic figure, not unlike his namesake. In keeping with an old scenic tradition, Oliveira makes him disappear or explode in a puff of smoke near the end of the film (Baecque and Parsi 92). Normally in scene with Niccolò at the same time, the narrator Iago serves a function much like Álvaro Carvalhal's narrator. Almost always facing and singing to the camera, he indicates at the outset that the story he is going to tell came his way via an anonymous manuscript titled "A True Story." He presents the characters, introduces the action, indicates what the personages are feeling, and points things out that the spectator might not be aware of. At one point, for example, he tells us that "an attentive observer can see, behind the curtain / two bloody eyes that seem to shoot bolts of lightning." The eyes belong to the covetous Dom João, who has a dagger in his hand. But since the story has not reached a point where the dagger might be useful, Iago sings, "Let's not dishonor ourselves. / Let's send the dagger back to the prop room."

Oliveira faithfully follows the narrative structure of Carvalhal's story, as summarized above. He divides it into two unequal parts, the first a gothic tragedy ending with the death of the Viscount, the second a cannibalistic farce ending with ferocious deglutition. The film opens, however, with typical Oliveirian self-reflexivity. During the credits superimposed on a black screen, we hear the sound of automobile traffic. The film's first image is of a Rolls Royce pulling up to the entranceway of a grand palace. As the doorman, dressed in sixteenth-century finery, opens the door, the door on the other side of the car also opens. When no one exits, he looks in. A point-of-view shot reveals the occupants—Niccolò and Iago—getting out on the other side and walking away. A countershot then shows the look of bewilderment on the doorman's face. Other cars and limos pull up, and a crowd applauds as the guests emerge, as if they were celebrities arriving for an Academy Awards ceremony. After the most important guests arrive, Niccolò begins playing his violin, and Iago sings his introduction to the "true story" we are about to see.

The first part of *Os Canibais* introduces the main characters during an aristocratic ball at a palatial estate, and it sets up the romantic triangle that never fully works itself out, except in death. As the ball begins, Margarida, dressed in white, seems somewhat sad as she anxiously awaits the arrival of a yet-to-be identified person. The narrator identifies her as a woman "who irresistibly provokes passion" in all men who see her. Dom João, however, speaks about her to the Baron (António Loja Neves). Since she is a woman, and he is a Don Juan, he feels that she must be ready to give in. The Baron, however, discourages him, saying that she is a woman who will give her heart only once, and that she is in love with the Viscount.

Midway through the ball, the mysterious Viscount is announced, and he slowly enters the room, walking somewhat stiffly. A female chorus—representing the sotto voce gossip that races around the room—asks, "What will he say? What will he do? What will he bring? What will happen?" The chorus also provides additional information about him, singing that he seems straight out of Byron, that he has been in America and Brazil, that he has rivers of money, that he sings like an angel, and that he does not want to marry. In their initial encounter, Margarida asks why he is always so sad, and he responds that he is unable to feign joys that are so distant from him. Their entire conversation is underlined by foreboding. The Viscount, famous for his arias, is soon asked to perform, and he sings of the nymph Echo, who faded away except for her voice, which was only able to repeat what others said.

After dinner and the ball, where Margarida and the Viscount dance the waltz, they and their guests retire to their rooms. Dom João, however, goes outside, where he pursues his plan to kill his rival. While he waits, pistol in hand, for the right moment, Margarida and the Viscount have their fateful conversation against the backdrop of a roaring fire in the fireplace, and Oliveira shoots a significant number of the Viscount's lines with him reflected in a cracked, concave distorting mirror that makes him look even more anguished and unworldly than he previously had. The fire, which in one shot frames even Margarida, serves as a visual metaphor for the impending destruction.

The Portuguese critic Fausto Cruchinho suggests that the Viscount sees in his inhuman body "the fulfillment of a new scientific spirit—half-man, half-machine. Once freed from its instinctive impulses the body can obtain a higher intellectual and aesthetic level, prophesying the advent of a new ethic that surpasses the human" (67). Nevertheless, despite his wealth, fame, and talent, because of his inhuman nature he is unable to love, since no woman will accept him. In their garden conversation where their first kiss took place he forewarns Margarida, because he knows of the probable consequences. But she does not understand, and she promises to follow him even if her nuptial bed is in the cemetery. On their wedding night he asks if she remembers her promises, and she responds that she has promised many things. After she rejects him and he rolls into the flames, the Viscount sings: "Go tell that ingrate that the mouth that sang the melodies that inebriated her is burning in the flames that she herself stoked." In other words, his death is the result of the love that she initiated and pursued, despite his warnings.

The Viscount and Margarida again embody the theme of frustrated love that runs throughout much of Oliveira's work. Margarida, who is of a somewhat lower social standing, is young, beautiful, and romantic, and she has apparently been successful in winning the heart of a wealthy and powerful man. The wedding night should be the culmination of their love. What happens, however, inverts this melodramatic model. In this marriage of the beauty and the beast, the beast does not become a handsome prince; he is truly inhuman, and their love is impossible. Their untouched bed becomes a symbol of that impossibility. As in other Oliveira films, amorous desire cannot be fulfilled through the body because "it belongs to the spirit, not the senses" (Cruchinho 67, 72).

Perhaps ironically, the tragic nuptial sequence also prepares the way for the farcical segment that follows. When the Viscount opens his robe and says, "Love me like I am," followed by the shot of his limbs dropping off onto the floor, the tragedy becomes a sort of tragicomedy. Although slight at this point, the shift in tone is reinforced when Dom João enters the room, sees the Viscount burning, and then almost trips over the limbs lying on the floor. He picks them up and leans them carefully against the wall beside the fireplace.

Unlike the first two parts of *Os Canibais*, which are nocturnal, the final segment takes place in broad daylight. It is in this segment that the film's title becomes clear. As in Carvalhal's tale, after their noble repast Margarida's father and one of her brothers pounce upon the magistrate brother "like starving mastiffs upon the tough skin of a Lamego ham." Oliveira visualizes this crucial moment by having the magistrate dressed as a pig and the father and his other son as wild hounds. But the director expands on the short story's ending by having all of the other characters—wedding guests, servants, and even a priest—bare their fangs and join in the feast. Niccolò plays while they devour, until he explodes in a puff of smoke. The pig then picks up his violin and plays a lively song while all of the others dance in circles around him. Margarida and Dom João even rise from the dead to join in the fun.

Oliveira's farcical comment about society as based on essentially cannibalistic relations recalls what Brazilian director Joaquim Pedro

Os Canibais (Cinemateca Portuguesa).

de Andrade wrote in relation to his 1969 film, *Macunaíma:* "[W]ork relationships, as well as . . . relationships between people—social, political, and economic—are still basically cannibalistic. Those who can, 'eat' others through their consumption of productions or even more directly in sexual relationships. Cannibalism has merely institutionalized, cleverly disguised itself" (82–83).[18] In the final analysis, however, Oliveira's film is much more about form and about cinematic possibilities than it is about politics, which would be central to his next feature. As a final note, *Os Canibais* is the first Oliveira film to feature Leonor Silveira, here in the role of Margarida. She would appear in all of the director's subsequent feature-length films except *O Dia do Desespero, A Caixa, O Quinto Império,* and *Belle Toujours.*

In the 1980s, Oliveira also made four documentaries: "Lisboa Cultural" (Cultural Lisbon; 1983), "Nice—À Propos de Jean Vigo" (Nice—about Jean Vigo; 1983), "Simpósio Internacional de Escultura em Pedra—Porto 1985" (International symposium of stone sculpture—Porto 1985; 1985), and "A Propósito da Bandeira Nacional" (About the national flag; 1987). "Lisboa Cultural" forms part of a series on the cultural capitals of Europe, produced by the Rome-based Trans World Film and intended for airing on television. Its coproducers were Italian and Portuguese television, RAI and RTP, respectively. Oliveira was not asked specifically for a film on Lisbon, but rather on an unspecified Portuguese city. He wavered between his native Porto and the country's capital and finally opted for the latter because he felt that it was more universal and would better represent the country as a whole (Oliveira 6).

In "Nice—À Propos de Jean Vigo," which forms part of a series of films made for television called *Regards sur la France,* Oliveira renders homage to French filmmaker Jean Vigo, and particularly his 1930 film, *À propos de Nice.* Although the two directors never met—Vigo died in 1934—their careers began at about the same time. Oliveira has stated that he admires the French director primarily because of his irreverence (Baecque and Parsi 95). In this documentary, Oliveira combines footage from Vigo's film with footage that he himself shot in Nice, both of the city and, more specifically, of Portuguese immigrants living there who offer their perspective. The film also includes brief segments with Oliveira's son, plastic artist Manoel Casimiro, who had been living in Nice since 1975, with intellectual Eduardo Lourenço, and with Vigo's daughter (Matos-Cruz 116).[19]

"Simpósio Internacional de Escultura em Pedra" and "A Propósito da Bandeira Nacional" both deal with art. The former, codirected by Manoel Casimiro, documents the process through which works of art emerge from blocks of stone, as sixteen sculptors prepare for an international sculpture symposium held in Porto in 1985. The latter focuses on an exhibit of Casimiro's paintings of Portugal's national flag, which the artist intended as a form of "painting of intervention" (Baecque and Parsi 101).

Bonfire of Vanities

Starting in 1990, Manoel de Oliveira entered the most productive period of his career, making at least one feature film per year. It is a particularly rich period, with such brilliant and moving films as *Abraham's Valley, Voyage to the Beginning of the World, I'm Going Home,* and *A Talking Picture.* In the films of this period Oliveira recasts some of the concerns he expressed in earlier films and explores new themes such as memory, death, aging and identity, nationhood and empire, and the state of civilization in the post-9/11 world in works that have consolidated his position as one of the great modern directors.

Non ou a Vã Glória de Mandar

At the end of the fourth canto of *The Lusiads* (1572), Luís de Camões's epic glorification of the Portuguese nation and its voyages of discovery, Vasco da Gama tells the Sultan of Malindi of his fleet's departure from Lisbon in July 1497 on its voyage to India. As they are leaving, an old man "of venerable appearance," the Velho do Restelo, criticizes the undertaking as being the result of greed and vanity and warns of the dangers that lie ahead.

> O pride of power! O futile lust
> For that vanity known as fame!
> That hollow conceit which puffs itself up
> And which popular cant calls honour!
> What punishment, what poetic justice,
> You exact on souls that pursue you!
> To what deaths, what miseries you condemn
> Your heroes! What pains you inflict on them! (95)

The stanza's first line in Portuguese is "Ó glória de mandar, ó vã cobiça." Translated literally, it would be, "Oh glory of command, oh vain avarice." Oliveira shifted the adjective "vain" from "avarice" to the "glory of command," thus using a variation on the Velho do Restelo's admonition, plus the Latin word "Non," taken from a sermon by Jesuit António Vieira (1608–97), to form the title of a film he had been thinking about since the time of the 1974 Portuguese Revolution.

Non ou a Vã Glória de Mandar (No or the vain glory of command; 1990) returns to questions of empire that Oliveira first addressed in *Le Soulier de satin* and that he would take up again in *A Talking Picture* (2003) and *O Quinto Império* (2004). It is a film about Portuguese history, and more specifically about some of the great battles of that history. The twist here is that the focus is not on Portuguese victories but rather on its defeats: the Lusitanians by the Romans (139 BC), King Afonso V at the hands of the Castillians in the Battle of Toro (1476), the failure to unify the Iberian Peninsula under Portuguese rule through the marriage of Prince Afonso and the Infanta Doña Isabel (1490), and the greatest loss of all, the battle of Alcácer-Kebir (1578), when the young and obsessive King Sebastian disappeared in northern Africa in a failed crusade for imperial expansion, resulting in sixty years of Spanish domination. Oliveira has described his film as the opposite of *The Lusiads,* with its exaltation of empire and nationhood (Baecque and Parsi 183). In many ways it echoes the voice of the Velho do Restelo cited above.

The film begins with a black screen and somber music on the soundtrack. Superimposed on the darkness is a line from António Vieira—"*Non* is a terrible word"—followed by the film's title. The opening take is a two-and-a-half-minute traveling shot around a tall, majestic tree in the African countryside, with the somber music replaced by an African percussion motif. The tree gives the sense of something mythical, eternal, and enigmatic, something that transcends the designs of men. As Thierry Jousse has put it, the tree represents a "core of ultimate and unbreakable resistance . . . an incarnation of obscure forces" (23). But they are forces that confirm life and stability, not death and conquest.

The film narrates in flashbacks a succession of historical events as told by a lieutenant in the Portuguese army in Angola during the country's colonial wars in Africa, wars that contributed greatly to the 1974 revolution because of the dissatisfaction it caused among military ranks. In this sense, its structure is not unlike that of *The Lusiads,* in which much of Portugal's history is told through narrative flashbacks, such as Vasco da Gama's narration to the Sultan of Malindi in cantos 3 and 4. Near the beginning of the film, as a small detachment of soldiers rides on an open truck through the African brush, one of them asks a question that the film attempts to answer: "What are we doing here?" The soldiers offer immediate and perhaps obvious responses: patriotism and the defense of the overseas provinces, the defense of the rights of peoples, nation building, or, contrarily, the indirect defense of the economic and political interests of the great powers. Oliveira's film offers a longer view, which takes shape as one of the soldiers, Lieutenant Cabrita, begins to tell his fellow soldiers of episodes in Portuguese history.

Oliveira establishes a sense of continuity in these episodes through the use of the same actors in the different historical battles. Luís Miguel Cintra, for example, plays Lieutenant Cabrita in the colonial war in Angola, as well as Viriato, a soldier in the Battle of Toro, and both Alex-

Luís Miguel Cintra as Lieutenant Cabrita in *Non*
(Cinemateca Portuguesa).

andre Moreira and D. João de Portugal in the Alcácer-Kebir sequence.
Diogo Dória plays the soldier Manuel, a Lusitanian warrior, a soldier
in the Battle of Toro, and the cousin of D. João de Portugal in Alcácer-
Kebir. The same goes for the other main actors. Significantly, they do
not appear in the two episodes that do not involve armed conflict. The
continuity, therefore, involves conquest through the force of arms.

Between a discussion among the soldiers in Africa on the fate of
empires and the film's reconstruction of the battle of Alcácer-Kebir, *Non
ou a Vã Glória de Mandar* offers an important moment of *The Lusiads*:
the episode of the Isle of Love from cantos 9 and 10 in which Venus,
who has protected the Portuguese from the beginning of their voyage,
wants to recompense them for their courage. To this end, she prepares a
"divine island" in the middle of the ocean where Vasco da Gama and his
sailors can have a few moments of pleasure in the company of beautiful
nymphs. The episode stands out from the rest of the film in several ways.

First, it is the only one that does not deal with death or defeat; rather, it depicts an earthly paradise of sensual pleasures. Second, it is the only flashback reconstructed according to a fictional source rather than historical documents. Finally, with the exception of Cabrita's agonizing delirium at the end of the film, it is the only episode that takes place on the level of myth rather than that of history.

Since it deals with myth, Oliveira's mise-en-scène in this episode does not adhere to the naturalist aesthetic that dominates the rest of the film, and this is no doubt a function of his respect for his source texts. In the other episodes he attempts to reconstruct historical events based on the information provided by specific historical documents, whereas in the Isle of Love episode he maintains a certain faithfulness to the poetic text of Luís de Camões, including the presence of little winged boys or Cupid's helpers, beautiful nymphs, and Venus, who descends from on high seated on a giant shell lowered by swans.[20] There is no dialogue during the episode, but the musical soundtrack includes the singing of selected verses from the two cantos in question. The final selection is the stanza in canto 10 in which the gods are demystified as products of the human imagination, "dreamed by mankind in his blindness" and useful "only to fashion delightful verses" (82).

This segment, which implicitly praises Portuguese voyages of discovery, would seem to contradict the rest of the film, since violence and conquest in the name of the nation and the Catholic church formed an inevitable part of those adventures. However, Lieutenant Cabrita puts the voyages in perspective when he tells his fellow soldiers that they are one of Portugal's great gifts to the world in that they opened way for more exploration and the development of human possibilities, just as space exploration and journeys to the moon have done more recently. In this sense, the voyages of discovery have a transcendent meaning. Those who are rewarded on the Isle of Love are the voyagers, the explorers, the discoverers, not the warriors; the actors who play soldiers are not present in the sequence. The gift of discovery is being praised, not the desire for conquest.[21] The question of demystification is particularly important, since the following historical episode deals with the disaster at Alcácer-Kebir.

Oliveira sets up the episode by first having Lieutenant Cabrita explain to his fellow soldiers the myth of the Fifth Empire, that is, the myth, propagated by Jesuit António Vieira and others, of an empire that would rule the world with a single monarch and a single pope. As Cabrita explains, Vieira referred to the Fifth Empire as the "consummation of the Empire of Christ on earth," which would last a thousand years until the coming of the antichrist. This messianic, mythical, universal, Catholic empire would convert heretics, Muslims, pagans, and Jews, resulting in a world of peace and harmony. It was, in short, a utopian vision for world domination, a vision that is "latent in the ambitions of the great powers, such as Russia and America."

The myth, Cabrita continues, took full shape with the death of King Sebastian in northern Africa. Midway through his recounting of the battle of Alcácer-Kebir, Cabrita receives orders for his troops to go out on a mission the following morning. In a battle with rebels, Cabrita is gravely wounded. As he lies on the ground awaiting rescue, he says: "War is like this." Shortly thereafter, a wounded African combatant screams as he runs through the brush holding his intestines. The battle continues until the sound of gunfire is replaced by silence, and the rebels have disappeared into the forest, carrying their dead and wounded.

The final sequence takes place in an army hospital, and it draws a clear parallel between the debacle of Alcácer-Kebir and the war in Angola. The sequence's opening shot is of a fan spinning round, its circularity echoing the circularity of the film's opening shot as well as numerous other circular images throughout the film. Then the camera initiates a slow horizontal tracking shot of wounded soldiers lying silently in their beds. It stops on a soldier whose entire head is covered with bandages, except for his right eye. After a brief shot of a doctor and his aide taking notes, the camera again focuses, this time in a close shot, on the bandaged man, his eye observing what transpires in front of him. Then, drawn by his groans and unconscious speech, it cuts to Lieutenant Cabrita, lying seriously wounded in his bed. He utters words about the "unexplained final meaning" as the film cuts to shots of devastation on the battleground of Alcácer-Kebir, where the same actor—Luís Miguel Cintra—is seen as a wounded D. João of Portugal. He says, "We have paid a high price for this adventure." D. João's words obviously refer both to King Sebastian's adventure in northern African and to the colonial occupation of Angola and other African nations.

At that point, a wounded Portuguese knight stands up and utters a tenebrous discourse that begins with the words from the Jesuit António Vieira that serve as the film's epigraph: "*Non* is a terrible word. It has no front or back. From whatever side you take it, it always sounds and says the same. Read it from beginning to end, or from end to beginning, it is always *non*. . . . It kills hope, which is Nature's ultimate remedy for all evils." The man then kills himself with his own sword. "Non," a kind of absolute negative, thus becomes an unredeemable sign of violence and death, a sign extending to all colonial ventures, not only those of Portugal.

The wounded Cabrita continues in agony, unsure where he is. He is in obvious pain, and the doctor orders a shot of morphine. He closes his eyes, and soft violin music begins on the soundtrack. In an image from Cabrita's unconscious, King Sebastian comes out of the fog by the Tagus River in Lisbon. In a medium shot, he unsheathes his sword, turns it upside down, and holds it close to his chest. After another brief shot of Cabrita, the camera focuses on King Sebastian's torso, with the inverted sword held upright in front of him as if a cross. Blood begins to run down his hands and drip off the tip of the sword. The film cuts back to Cabrita, who opens his eyes, and then back, as if in a countershot, to King Sebastian, who gazes toward the camera.

Cabrita begins jerking convulsively and vomits blood. The doctors rush to help, giving him adrenaline and pumping his chest. The single, unbandaged eye of the other wounded soldier looks on. An extreme close-up of the eye reveals a terribly frightened gaze filling the screen. As João Bénard da Costa has written, the eye expresses "total, absolute intensity, as if only it could see and knew how to see, the only possible point of view on what takes place in the infirmary filled with heat and blood. One would need to go back to Buñuel's *Un Chien Andalou* to recall such an unsettling image of an eye" ("'Non'" 1). The doctors finally give up, and we see a close shot of medical log, on which a hand holding a pen begins to write. As it writes, entering Cabrita's death in the log, Manoel de Oliveira himself says in a voiceover: "Lieutenant Cabrita died on the day of the April 25, 1974, Revolution." The pen is laid to rest on the log as the credits being to roll, accompanied by Teresa Salgueiro (the lead singer of Madredeus) singing Venus's words from the Isle of Love episode, in which she asks her son Cupid to help her prepare a recompense for the Portuguese because of the many hardships they have endured.[22]

Sebastian and Cabrita both represent the end of an era: Sebastian the end of Portugal's period of conquest in the name of Christ (thus the bloody, inverted sword), Cabrita the end of modern Portuguese colonialism. The Revolution of 1974 dramatically brings the latter to a close and points toward a different future. That, of course, does not mean that ambitions for power and domination on the part of other nations no longer exist, and this is a matter that Oliveira takes up later in his career, particularly in *A Talking Picture*.

A Divina Comédia

After discussing issues related to conquest and colonialism, specifically in relation to the history of Portugal, in *Non*, Manoel de Oliveira turned his attention toward the whole of western civilization in *A Divina Comédia* (The divine comedy; 1992). Despite its title, the film is not an adaptation of Dante, nor does Dante figure directly among its literary references. Oliveira's divine comedy draws from a number of sources: the Bible, José Régio's play *A Salvação do Mundo* (1954), Dostoevsky's *Crime and Punishment* and *The Brothers Karamazov*, and Nietzsche's *Anti-Christ*. According to Oliveira, all of the texts he uses deal in some way with the problem of sin and the possibility of redemption, and in this sense they all derive ultimately from the same source (see the interview "A Mental Conception of Cinema," in this volume).

The film's setting is an insane asylum (Casa de Alienados), although, as João Bénard da Costa has observed, it seems more like the elegant manor of *O Passado e o Presente* than what one might think of as a mental institution ("Pedra" 12). Its characters are drawn from diverse biblical and literary sources (or at least they assume biblical and literary identities), and they interact in this timeless drama as if in an eternal present. From the Bible are Adam and Eve, Jesus and Lazarus, Mary and Martha, and the Pharisee. Four figures—Sonya and Raskolnikov and Ivan Karamazov and his brother Alyosha—come from Dostoevsky (as do, in brief and fatal roles, Alyona Ivanova and her sister Lizaveta). The film also includes a prophet, drawn from José Régio's above-mentioned play, and a skeptical and sarcastic philosopher whose arguments come straight from Nietzsche.

To complicate matters, the actors may represent one or more characters. Leonor Silveira, for example, plays Eve at the outset but then convinces herself that she is Saint Teresa, much to Adam's dismay. The pianist Maria José Pires plays the biblical Martha, and yet early in the film the asylum director tells another character that it is Maria José Pires who is at the piano. In one case, two actors play the same character—the asylum director—although that was not part of the director's original intent. Ruy Furtado became ill before they completed shooting, and Oliveira chose to take his place as a form of homage rather than replace him with another actor. It is Oliveira, not Furtado, who interacts with the Karamazov brothers during their key conversation.

A *Divina Comédia* does not have a dramatic plot per se; its conflicts are clashes of ideas. It advances polyphonically through a series of extensive dialogues, generally between pairs of characters: the prophet (Luís Miguel Cintra) and the philosopher (Mário Viegas), Sonya and Raskolnikov, and the Karamazov brothers and the asylum director (during which Ivan reads segments from "The Grand Inquisitor"). At the same time, the film reenacts key scenes from its sources: Adam and Eve in the Garden of Eden, the Last Supper, Raskolnikov's double murder (which takes place in an expressionist dream sequence that evokes Wiene's *The*

Maria José Pires in *A Divina Comédia*
(Cinemateca Portuguesa).

Cabinet of Dr. Caligari), Lazarus's resurrection, the kiss between Ivan and Alyosha, and Raskolnikov's repentance. Although this may suggest the use of *tableaux vivants*, as in *Le Soulier de satin*, that is not the case. All of the characters represent their literary or biblical identities and their status as "patients" at the same time, and one scene or dialogue flows naturally—to the extent that is possible—into the next, within the confines of the house or its grounds.

The film opens, for example, with an establishing shot of the manor where the action takes place. Then, inside the house, a young woman (Maria de Medeiros) runs down a dark hallway, calling out for Raskolnikov (Miguel Guilherme). He comes out of his room, asking Sonya what is happening, and they both rush over to a window. Outside, beside a tree laden with fruit, Adam (Carlos Gomes) and Eve (Silveira) stand naked under a tree. Eve picks an apple, takes a bite, and offers it to Adam. Near the asylum, the director and an assistant look on, as do the institution's patients, including Sonya and Raskolnikov, from a nearby window. Outside again, thunder and lightning begin to strike. The assistant goes inside to get an umbrella, while Adam and Eve cower in the rain. Another assistant brings out two red robes (red perhaps representing the color of transgression), and as he moves toward the naked couple a snake slithers away in the grass.

As Adam and Eve are taken back to the house, the film cuts to the group of onlookers inside, who back away from the window. A young man (Paulo Matos)—who later assumes the role of Jesus—steps out from the others and speaks from Genesis 3, ending with "for dust you are / and to dust you will return." A woman, meanwhile, runs down a hallway, kneels before a painting of Christ, and prays. A number of elements are obviously in play here. Through the mention of the names of Sonya and Raskolnikov and the reenactment of Adam and Eve in the Garden of Eden, followed by the biblical words of God and the woman in prayer, *A Divina Comédia* begins with the question of transgression and ends with a plea for redemption, as Raskolnikov, accompanied by Sonya, does penance by walking on his knees around the circular driveway in front of the asylum. And yet, even at the end Oliveira does not provide a clear answer to the questions raised, which are always open to spectator interpretation.

O Dia do Desespero

Some critics see Oliveira's next film, *O Dia do Desespero* (Day of despair; 1992), as a relatively minor work in the broader scope of his filmography. In his chronological study of Oliveira's work, which includes sometimes extensive analyses, René Prédal offers only five paragraphs (plus one sentence) on the film, referring to it as "un film muséal" (a museum film), placing his discussion out of sequence, after *Francisca* (63). Jacques Lemière notes that the film was not well received in either France or Portugal (125–26). I would suggest, and Lemière would agree, that *O Dia do Desespero,* which at seventy-five minutes is one of the director's shortest features, is in fact a small masterpiece. A film about death, it is perhaps Oliveira's most spectral and phantasmagoric film, a film in which the final words come from the grave.

O Dia do Desespero returns to the figure of Camilo Castelo Branco, the author of *Amor de Perdição* and a character in *Francisca.* Oliveira has said that in Portugal there is no greater parallel to what Cervantes's Don Quijote represents in Spain than Camilo Castelo Branco, "not so much for his work or for any of his characters, but rather for the person himself . . . and the drama of his life, his desire for a 'marriage' with the Spirit, if not to say with Death" ("Dom Quichote"). Based largely on the writer's letters, *O Dia do Desespero* deals with his final days and suicide in 1890 and, perhaps more importantly, with the way in which Camilo's story is told. Indeed, Camilo and his companion Ana Plácido appear relatively little in the film, and Camilo only appears seated at his desk. The actress Teresa Madruga, however, is an almost constant visual presence as herself.

Most of the film was shot in the house—now a museum—where Camilo lived the last years of his life and where he killed himself shortly after learning that his increasing blindness was irreversible. The camera lingers on some of the many paintings and portraits in the house, and Teresa Madruga gives us a brief "tour." Despite such ostensibly "documentary" elements, *O Dia do Desespero* is a fictional film; but, according to Oliveira, it is one that refuses to deceive the spectator by pretending to be what it is not (Baecque and Parsi 56). Even the use of Teresa Madruga as herself cannot be considered "real," since we do not see the actress as she really is but rather as she appears in Oliveira's film.

In this sense, she too is phantasmatic. In *O Dia do Desespero* and other films, Manoel de Oliveira questions the ontological status of such terms as "fiction" and "documentary" and challenges, through the pursuit of his own cinematic vision, some of the filmic and narrative conventions that have come to dominate mainstream commercial cinema, including the transparency of much cinematic discourse.

Midway through the credits, the film's first image is a static, fifty-second shot of a pen-and-ink portrait of the novelist. After the credits end, the camera focuses on a block of paper on a desk. A man's hands come into view, and he picks up a pen. The shot is interrupted by an intertitle that briefly explains Camilo's relationship with Bernardina Amélia, a daughter born of one of his many affairs who maintained esteem for the writer, even though he had long since abandoned her mother. The hand that picked up the pen begins to write, and another intertitle appears with a citation from Virgil: "Can anger black as this prey on the minds of heaven?"

There follows one of those shots that is quintessential Oliveira: a four-and-a-half-minute high-angle shot of a carriage wheel rolling along a dirt road, while a male voiceover reads passages from letters the novelist wrote to his daughter. We do not see who is in the carriage, nor do we know where it is going. Its dramatic function has less to do with a specific action than with its metaphorical sense. The words we hear talk about illness, the difficulty the writer has in traveling to Porto, the long journey of life, and, finally, death. Visually, the take recalls the long traveling shot that opens *Non ou a Vã Glória de Mandar*, and it anticipates the dominant visual motif of *Voyage to the Beginning of the World* (1997). The camera is static, fixed on the side of the carriage looking down at the wheel, and yet the shot is not motionless because of the movement of the wheel, the unevenness of the road, the play of light and shadows, and the rhythm of the narrator's voice. Responding to the suggestion that the shot is hallucinatory or hypnotic, Oliveira responds, "Yes it is hallucinatory. It's a turning wheel, but it is also many other things: there is the movement, the gravitation that suspends the stars. . . . The wheel that turns is life. . . . It moves up and down like the wheel of fortune. There is a dramatic sense to it because during the shot light and velocity change. There are moments when the wheel goes faster, others, in the most dramatic moments, when it almost stops, like when we approach or become more distant from death. It is absolutely not just the mechanical play of a wheel rolling along to the same rhythm, in the same light, like the wheel of a machine, for example" (Baecque and Parsi 143–44). This comment points toward an important aspect of Oliveira's view of the cinema, which he expresses in diverse ways in different films. Even a shot of an object that may seem purely mechanical potentially carries a psychological or existential meaning that transcends the object itself. The spinning wheel obviously denotes a journey, although we may not know who is undertaking that journey, but its circularity is also metaphorical. Like life itself, its velocity changes, as does the terrain on which it rolls and the light and shadows that illuminate or cast a shadow over it. In other words, there is human drama in the very object and its motion, a drama that magnifies the words of the voiceover.

As the voiceover narration comes to an end, the image shifts to a man seated at a desk by a window. The spectator might expect that the man is Camilo Castelo Branco and that the "story" will begin. However, the man stands up, faces the camera, and introduces himself as the actor Mário Barroso. He says that he will be playing the role of Camilo and briefly talks about the writer. Barroso, who is also the film's cinematographer, played Camilo in *Francisca*. Framed by oval photographs of Camilo and Ana Plácido, Teresa Madruga, the actress who plays Ana Plácido, introduces herself in much the same manner and provides some history about Ana Plácido's relationship with Camilo.

Although they had been in a relationship for some time, a scandal broke out when it became public in 1857. Ana Plácido soon left her husband for Camilo, and they had their first child in 1859. The following year, Ana Plácido's husband had them arrested. Camilo was imprisoned in the same jail in Porto in which his uncle, Simão Botelho, had been held in the early 1800s for killing his rival for the hand of Teresa de Albuquerque, and it was there that Camilo wrote *Amor de Perdição* based on their story. Teresa Madruga points out the parallelism between the two love affairs. Suddenly, she hears a male voice calling her name. The voice is not calling her, however, but rather Teresa de Albuquerque from Camilo's novel. Madruga and Barroso, whose voice we heard, then "become" Teresa de Albuquerque and Simão, using words from Camilo's novel. Accompanied by somber music, the scene takes on remarkable dramatic intensity, while at the same time rendering more complex the question of representation and identity in the film.

Almost a third into the film, we finally see Camilo at his desk composing a letter about his son's madness, and the scene is intercut with expressionistic shots of his son, who hallucinates at a window, his moves mimicking those of the distorted trees twisting in the wind outside. Again we see Camilo at his desk, but the film cuts to Teresa Madruga, who seems to be looking down at him, providing a broader context for part of the situation he is describing in the letter. In a subsequent shot of Camilo, Madruga enters the scene and stands by the window near Camilo's desk. From the beginning, conventional cinematic realism breaks down through the use of such distancing effects, with multiple temporalities and shifting relationships between actors and characters in play.

Earlier in the film, for example, Madruga mentions that one day Ana Plácido was working at her own desk when she sensed something happening on the floor above, where she and Camilo had separate bed-

Mário Barroso as Camilo in *O Dia do Desespero*
(Cinemateca Portuguesa).

rooms. The camera looks down the empty stairway. A countershot shows the stairway from below, and Ana Plácido enters the scene and goes up the stairs. The image cuts back to the second-floor landing, but it is Madruga as herself, not as Ana Plácido, who comes out onto the second floor. Somewhat later, it is Madruga as Ana Plácido, not as herself, who goes back down the staircase.

This play of identities reaches its paroxysm in a scene in which Ana Plácido is being dressed with the help of a servant. The first shot of the sequence shows her in a mirror, putting on makeup. She stands, and the servant helps her dress. She asks for a cigar and sits in a chair, where we see her on the right side of the screen and her mirror image on the left. A cut takes us to a medium shot of Ana Plácido in the mirror, looking directly at the camera and smoking the cigar. Suddenly, she takes off her wig, and it is no longer Ana Plácido we see but rather Teresa Madruga, who talks about a novel Ana Plácido wrote under a pseudonym—*Herança de Lágrimas* (Legacy of tears)—in which she cites, in French, George Sand, the male pseudonym of Amandine-Aurore-Lucile Dupin. Nothing is as it seems; everything is phantasmagoric.

The spectral nature of the film becomes even clearer because of the sound in two sequences in which Camilo writes at his desk. In the first, the background sound is similar to that of the carriage of the long sequence early in the film. In the second, illuminated by numerous candles, the sound is of the howling wind and howling wolves. Death surrounds him. In both, Camilo expresses increasing concern about his eyesight.

The film's denouement, Camilo's suicide, takes place off screen, and this has to do with Oliveira's deontological stance. Everything that Camilo says in the film is historically accurate (that is, he actually wrote everything that he says in the film), but it is impossible to know precisely how his suicide took place. The historical record apparently says nothing about the kind of gun he used, and he was alone when he killed himself. Ana Plácido accompanied the doctor (Diogo Dória) to the door, where they heard a gunshot. Oliveira limits himself to a shot of Camilo dead in his rocking chair, followed by another of the empty chair, and yet another of his cigar, still smoldering on the floor, smoke spiraling into the air. After Ana Plácido repeats to authorities (whom we do not see) the events we have just witnessed, the film's final shot is of Camilo's grave, with a tenebrous voiceover about the coldness of death and the difficulty of transforming flesh into dust.

Vale Abraão

For his next film, *Vale Abraão* (Abraham's valley; 1993), Oliveira again collaborates with the novelist Agustina Bessa-Luís, whose *Fanny Owen* served as the basis for *Francisca*.[23] Oliveira had wanted to film Flaubert's *Madame Bovary* with locations in Normandy, but the producer, Paulo Branco, did not think such a project would be viable, particularly since it would be very expensive and they could probably not count on financial support from the Portuguese film agency for what would essentially be a French film. The director then considered the possibility of transposing the story to Portugal, and he suggested that Bessa-Luís write her own version of Flaubert's novel set in Portugal rather than France, and in the present rather than the past (Baecque and Parsi 71). She did so, resulting in *Vale Abraão* (1991), but in her own inimitable meandering, digressive, labyrinthine style—which is anything but cinematic—and with no interference from Oliveira, who then wrote the screenplay and adapted it to film as he might any other novel.

Oliveira's *Abraham's Valley* is thus doubly palimpsestic, with *Madame Bovary* as an implicit subtext and an explicit presence: Ema (with one *m*) is nicknamed "Bovarinha" (Little Bovary), she reads Flaubert's novel, which Oliveira makes a point of showing in close-up, and at one point she and a male character discuss the nickname, which she adamantly rejects, saying that despite the similarity of her first name, she "is not Madame Bovary" (and indeed she is not). Like Flaubert's Emma, she marries a mediocre provincial doctor—Carlos, like Flaubert's Charles—whom she does not love, and she has several extramarital affairs before dying in an accident that may in fact be intentional and thus an act of suicide. As in Flaubert's novel, Ema's awakening to desire occurs at a ball given by the local *haute bourgeoisie*. Despite such similarities, there are many differences between *Madame Bovary* and Bessa-Luís's novel, starting from which Oliveira elaborates his own vision.

Abraham's Valley is set in the wine-producing Douro region of northern Portugal near the town of Lamego. The beautiful landscapes—terraced hillsides covered with vineyards, a winding, cliff-lined river, stately if somewhat decadent country manors—become almost another character as a backdrop for this lyrical portrayal of a woman's desire for romantic love and social ascension. Oliveira's camera sets the location and mood of the film through long, normally static establishing shots, while at the same time giving the spectator a sense of the region's great beauty.

Oliveira's Ema is played by two actresses. The Spanish actress Cécile Sanz de Alba plays Ema as a fourteen-year-old adolescent, and Leonor Silveira appears as Ema the adult. Ema's mother died when she was six, and she was raised by her hypochondriac father and her pious spinster Aunt Augusta. The film does not dwell on Ema's youth other than to provide a brief glimpse of the austere atmosphere of a decadent, conservative bourgeoisie in which she was raised, as well as a sense of her nascent sensuality.

Ema first meets Carlos Paiva (Luís Miguel Cintra) when she is fourteen and is having lunch with her father, Paulino Cardeano (Rui de Carvalho), in a restaurant in Lamego, where they have gone for the annual Festa dos Remédios. She finds him a simpleton, while at the same time recognizing that he speaks with a certain "masculine grace." They meet again some time later when he visits their home in Romesal. Ema is rather distant, if not outright rude, to the point that, as he leaves, Carlos thinks to himself, "Who does she think she is?"

The sequence following Carlos's visit is indicative of the tensions at play in Ema's life. As she looks out the window, the narrator speaks of her faint memories of her mother and particularly of the breast milk that they would drip in her ear when she had an earache. "The rest was a secret and hallucinatory kinship with the womb from which she had come, a room where sounds and words echoed, where everything moved with a comfortable elasticity." As the narrator speaks, Ema picks up and smells a red rose, sensually leaning her head back as she does, and she then fingers the inside of the flower in what has been described as one of the most erotic images of Portuguese cinema. She then picks up and opens a book that is lying on the table: it is *Madame Bovary.* Her aunt tells her that she should believe in God and pray more and that she should not be reading such books. She wants Ema to become a nun, to which Ema responds with derisive laughter. The scene effectively contrasts age and youth, religious piety and sensuality, conformity and an incipient rebelliousness. Although Ema's sensuality and desire become apparent in this sequence, she is unprepared, the narrator informs us after she encounters young vineyard workers, "to deal with obvious lust." That is not a problem with the family's maids, who comfortably engage in sexual banter with similar workers.

Some time later Ema's Aunt Augusta dies. During her wake, Carlos is called to Romesal to see one of the maids, Branca, who has fallen ill. It is during this visit that Ema, now played by Leonor Silveira, begins to take serious notice of Carlos, and their relationship begins. Its association with the atmosphere of death is anything but auspicious. Carlos had been married to a woman that Oliveira portrays in rather grotesque terms. When he returns home after having met Ema and her father at the restaurant, his wife is washing her feet and applying a yellow powder because of impetigo. Perhaps because of his demeanor or her intuition, she immediately senses that he has "seen someone." But between that time and Aunt Augusta's death, she too passes away, leaving Carlos free. Ema soon marries Carlos, although she recognizes that she doesn't love him. The close shot of Ema framed beside a birdcage is thus metaphorical.

After their marriage Ema seems happy, but Carlos is often out on

Leonor Silveira in *Abraham's Valley* (Cinemateca Portuguesa).

house calls, and because of frequent patient visits at night, he opts to sleep in a separate bedroom to avoid disturbing her sleep. She begins to feel abandoned. Her only solace is the maid Rita, a deaf mute who is the only servant who accompanies her from Romesal to her new home in Abraham's Valley. To relieve her glumness, Carlos decides to take her to Sunday mass at the manor of Maria de Loreto (Glória de Matos) and her husband Semblano (António Reis), one of the wealthiest families of the valley. During the mass, in which the voiceover is the homily, Oliveira reveals the pettiness and hypocrisy of those in attendance, who are more interested in seeing who is present and in looking down on Ema than in the words of the priest. Afterwards, the narrator tells us that Carlos's sisters found Ema frivolous and that Carlos had "fallen into the illegitimate infamy of investigating Ema's morals, but he found nothing wrong. She was as pure as the stars." While the narrator speaks of the judgmental attitude of Carlos's sisters and his infamy, Oliveira's camera focuses on a small statue of Christ on the oratory in Ema's house in Romesal, not so subtly pointing out the contrast between them.

The Jacas ball marks an important turning point in *Abraham's Valley*. As the narrator tells us, "Everything started when Carlos Paiva took her to the Jacas ball. He had an express invitation from the Lumiares who, in addition, took advantage of the occasion to get to know Ema, without committing themselves to accepting her." At the dance, she attracts the attention of some of the most important men of the valley, virtually none from her husband, and condescending glances from the women. She dances with Fernando Osório (Diogo Dória), and when he gets up from the sofa where he has been talking to Ema and Pedro Lumiares (Luís Lima Barreto), Ema furtively puts his cigarette case in her purse.

The following sequence—one of the few without a voiceover narration—represents a key moment in Ema's transformation. After returning from the Jacas ball, she is in her bedroom alone. The lights are off, and the room is illuminated only by moonlight coming in through the window. The initial shot of the sequence is a point-of-view shot looking out the window, the horizontal and vertical framing appearing as if bars keeping Ema cloistered. Dressed in a diaphanous pink silk nightgown and robe, she takes Fernando's cigarette case out of her purse and smells it, sensually leaning her head back in visual echo of the shot earlier in the film in which the adolescent Ema makes a similar and more erotically charged gesture with a rose. Ema rises from the chair in which she had been seated, looks in a mirror above the dresser, lights two candles, and again picks up and smells the cigarette pack. She then passes a candle around her face as if to warm or illuminate it. She blows one of the candles out, then leaves the room and walks down the stairs to her husband's bedroom. He opens the door, and she enters. Ema and Carlos stand before yet another mirror, but in their reflection, a candle separates them. The cigarette case and the candle become obvious symbols of desire, and desire for someone other than Carlos.

This sequence is also representative of Oliveira's use of music. For *Abraham's Valley* he chose two "moonlight" pieces, Debussy's "Clair de lune" and Beethoven's "Moonlight Sonata," to which he added music on a similar theme by Fauré, Strauss, and Schumann. He has said that he used Debussy for the more romantic or lyrical scenes and Beethoven for more somber or dramatic moments (Baecque and Parsi 175). In addition to contributing to a shot or sequence's tone and mood, the music also contributes to its meaning and, often, its duration. Oliveira will frequently allow a shot to continue until the end of the music he selected to accompany it. In such instances, the music determines the duration of the shot, not the dramatic necessity of the visual image. Right before the ball, for example, there is a shot of Rita washing clothes outdoors. Nothing else happens, there is no dialogue and no voiceover, yet the shot runs for almost a full minute until the accompanying music ends.

The five-plus-minute shot of Ema in her room is accompanied throughout by Debussy's "Clair de lune," which enhances its lyrical and romantic mood, musically reinforcing the image of moonlight coming through the window. The music continues while she goes downstairs, by candlelight, to her husband's room. It ends just as Ema and Carlos look in the mirror together, separated by a candle, the silence signaling the lack of romance in their relationship and prefiguring what is to come.

The passage of time is never precise in *Abraham's Valley*. It is marked by such things as the change of actresses in the lead role, changes in Ema's wardrobe and hairstyle, references to events such as her pregnancy, the appearance and growth of her two daughters, Lolota and Luisona, and Ema's succession of lovers. The film moves forward through sometimes extensive narrative blocks, often consisting of long dialogues or conversations among diverse characters that slowly offer information about changes in Ema's life or the reasons for and consequences of her actions, and we often learn of such things indirectly, through other characters or the narrator, rather than through Ema herself. We hear that she is pregnant, for example, in a conversation between Pedro and Simona Lumiares (Micheline Larpin). Ema's adultery is first suggested by the narrator, who tells us that Carlos sensed that she was about to do "something rash" and that he wanted to push her toward Pedro Lumiares, "a robot," but one with the advantage of knowing how to talk about love.

Abraham's Valley deals with love, but it is not a love story. It deals with adultery but, unlike *Madame Bovary,* not with scandal. Ema's transgressions seem to be accepted, even by her husband. Her decision to engage in an extramarital affair with Fernando Osório comes about in a matter-of-fact manner. The sequence opens with an external shot of a veranda, whose railings are covered with flowering vines, accompanied by Fauré's "Clair de lune." In a digressive discourse on verandas taken directly from Bessa-Luís's novel (56), as is most of the film's language, the narrator says, "They say that 'veranda' is a Celtic word that means 'barrier.' That may be true. We don't know why it has had such importance in rural and urban architecture. It's a kind of belly that demonstrates power and affected desire. It serves to court the world and to demonstrate an individual's status. It invites an appraising gaze that leads to sin, casting its shade over virginity. It is a place of leisure, more sensual than licentious."

As the narrator finishes his digression, the film cuts to a door. Two preadolescent girls come out onto the veranda, followed by Ema. In a chronological disjunction between narration and image, the voiceover tells us that "the veranda of Abraham's Valley was put to new use. Ema lived there, newborn daughters in her arms." Obviously, her daughters are not newborn, although this is the first time they are mentioned or seen. Ema's husband then comes out onto the veranda, and the girls go back inside. He asks if she is going to Vesúvio, the estate of Fernando Osório, and she responds that she is, saying that she needs to rest for a few days. It is clear, even by the red dress she is wearing, that her affair with Fernando has begun, not out of desire but rather provocation. The narrator describes her lover as a "defendant who has already been convicted."

Abraham's Valley also deals with sex, but in a chaste yet sensual manner. There is no nudity, and there is little if any overt affection shown between the film's characters. Ema is dissatisfied with her life, and she wants the kind of romantic love she has read about, but that is never a real possibility in Oliveira's films. She also wants admission into the region's high society, which is in part what leads to her affair with Fernando Osório. Like Flaubert's Emma, however, her transgressions lead to her downfall, which becomes clear when Caires, the former butler at Vesúvio, offers her money to sleep with him.

In *Abraham's Valley,* Oliveira returns to some of the cinematic strategies used in *Amor de Perdição* and *Francisca,* notably the creative use of a voiceover narration, with multiple variations in the relationship between sound and image, and the use of a largely static camera. Responding to critics who suggest that extensive use of an external narrative voice interferes with the action, Oliveira responds, "[I]t is not language that intrudes but rather the action. The film begins with language and uses language to tell the story" (Baecque and Parsi 91). It is the narration, not the image, that moves the plot forward.

The narrator is the film's cinematographer Mário Barroso, who played the role of the writer Camilo Castelo Branco in *Francisca* and *O Dia do Desespero.* His voice brings an additional level of intertextuality to the film. At times, the narration provides broad and specific contextualization. At the beginning of the film, for example, the narrator establishes not a geographical context but rather a moral context with biblical roots: "In Abraham's Valley, a land of people forced to confront their own pride, anger, and shame, things have happened, and continue to happen, that belong to the world of dreams, the most hypocritical world that exists. Abraham had an archaic custom: he would use the beauty of his wife, Sara, as a solution to his problems. He would say that she was his sister, which opened the way for other men's desire." At others, it offers pseudo-philosophical digressions, as on the social and metaphorical function of the veranda. In some cases, the narration is redundant in relation to the image, describing precisely what we see on screen, as when Ema enters the room during Carlos's first visit to their house in Romesal. In others, it contradicts the characters. In the same scene, Ema says that she does not remember Carlos; the omniscient narrator tells us that she does remember him and that she found him handsome, "with straight, white teeth." At yet other moments, it anticipates the image, telling us what we will soon see, as when Ema arrives for a visit with the judgmental Mello sisters.

After *Abraham's Valley*, Oliveira made three shorter feature-length films: *A Caixa* (The box; 1994), *The Convent* (1995), and *Party* (1996).[24] Ironically, although they are probably less significant in terms of his overall body of work, two of the three—*The Convent* and *Party*—have had wider international distribution than some of his more important films, with DVD versions available even in the United States. This is likely due to two factors: the greater accessibility of their cinematic discourse and the fact that they both feature international stars: Catherine Deneuve and John Malkovich in *The Convent,* and Irene Pappas and Michel Piccoli in *Party*.

A Caixa

A Caixa is based on a 1981 play by Helder Prista Monteiro. The story is simple. In a poor Lisbon neighborhood, a blind man (Luís Miguel Cintra) sits outside his house every morning selling needles, thread, erasers, and other odds and ends but, more importantly, hoping that passersby will put change in his "official" alms box. The box is official because it was granted to him by the Louis Braille Beneficent Association (thus the letters ABLB on the side of the box), which authorizes him to solicit money. During the day—and the film takes place during a single day—the unnamed blind man, who lives with his daughter and her husband, interacts with residents of the street and passersby.

The blind man is not really the film's protagonist, although in many ways he and his box represent its center. If *A Caixa* has a protagonist, it is the street where all of its action occurs: a narrow, pedestrian-only stairway in the shadow of a nearby church. Its residents are poor and, by their accent, probably rural in origin. They include an elderly woman who begins her day by urinating in the middle of the street, a pregnant woman, a prostitute, men who frequent a nearby tavern, and so forth. Also present on the street, but with little or no direct interaction with the blind man, are the tavern owner, a guitar player in the tavern, a woman who sells chestnuts, another who carries her easel out into the street to paint an urban scene, and two obnoxious American tourists who find everything quite "picturesque."

The alms box of the title is structurally significant in that it is generally the focus of attention. The blind man's son-in-law is the box's guardian when he is not on the street. Several characters tell the blind man that they would like to have a box so that they could also collect money from passersby. He responds defensively that they can't have one because they are not blind. At one point, some of the men who frequent the tavern take the box and toss it back and forth, leaving the blind man near panic. The drama intensifies when the box is stolen and a second blind man—who is not really blind—appears on the street with his own box. The denouement is one of violence: the son-in-law becomes involved in a fight, kills another man, and is arrested, thus effectively abandoning his wife, and the blind man apparently kills himself with a knife, distraught by the loss of his box and an argument with his daughter.

Much of the film is shot in a realist mode, with the limitations inherent in its theatrical source and the extremely restricted spaces—the street and the tavern—in which the drama plays out. But Oliveira is not content with such a limited reading, and his film quickly points in directions not indicated by Monteiro's play, often in either a highly ironic or a sublimely poetic manner, particularly through his use of music. The opening sequence delineates the dramatic space as, in the early morning

Luís Miguel Cintra as the blind man in *A Caixa*
(Cinemateca Portuguesa).

hours, an inebriated night watchman staggers along the street, swigging as he goes. As he reaches the stairway, the sounds of Stravinsky's "Song of the Volga Boatmen" softly begins on the soundtrack. The music increases in volume and satirical intensity as he struggles to make it to the top, and it continues, somewhat lower in volume, as he exits left in the direction indicated by a sign on the wall that says "Theater." His ascent and exit are followed by several low-angle shots of the imposing façade of a church that overlooks the stairway and those who live along it. Oliveira's irony continues, although on a somewhat lighter note, with the use of Katchaturian's "Sabre Dance" accompanying a flood of city residents rushing up and down the stairway on their way to work.

Two musical interludes in *A Caixa* stand out for their sublimity. The first poetic sequence takes place in the tavern, away from the main action, prior to the theft of the box that sets the tragic events in motion. The sequence involves two people, the tavern owner (Rui de Carvalho) and a man with a guitar (Duarte Costa). The owner asks the man about his instrument, since he is used to hearing the guitar played merely as an accompaniment to the *fado*. When the man plays, however, it sounds like an orchestra. The man responds that he is not a *fadista* but a music teacher, and for him the guitar represents a form of relief from the injustices, betrayals, and disillusionments of the world. He has distanced himself from a world he does not like. The owner says that he would like to hear something "fine" or elegant, and the musician then plays Schubert's "Ave Maria," temporarily transforming the tavern into a place of beauty and solace that the imposing church up the hill does not offer. As he plays, the camera focuses on his dirty hands, as if to suggest that beauty depends on aesthetic sensibility, not on social class or the vagaries of fortune. Lest the spectator get carried away and too absorbed in this moment of peace and reflection, the film cuts back to the stairway outside as a female painter leaves her house with an easel, clumsily carrying it down the stairs until she finds an appropriate place to paint, while the music continues in the background. Soon the music is interrupted by the blind man's screams: his box has been stolen.

Between the film's dramatic denouement, when the daughter finds that her blind father has stabbed himself, and the epilogue, Oliveira's camera focuses on the empty stairway. The lighting changes to blue, and a group of ballet dancers emerges and dances to the sounds of

Ponchielli's "Dance of the Hours" from the opera *La Gioconda*. This beautiful sequence provides poetic relief from the tragic events of the drama. Here, however, we are very distant from an ideal city, which makes artistic expression all the more important. But things may not be that simple. As the film's epigraph states, although *A Caixa* "takes place as the reality of a poor, popular neighborhood, it is really no more than the age-old fable of anachronisms and social differences in today's world." The epigraph clearly points toward a metaphor for the world that transcends national boundaries, but Saguenail and Regina Guimarães have suggested that the film also offers an allegory of contemporary Portugal and the "state of mendicancy" in which it finds itself during the period of integration into the European Union. Indeed, the ballerinas, dressed in gold tutus and dancing in the blue light of the street, form what appears to be the flag of the EU, which Oliveira has described as a utopian gesture toward unity.

O Convento

In *The Convent* (1995), starring Catherine Deneuve and John Malkovich, Oliveira turns toward the Faustian theme of good and evil. It is his third film based on or inspired by the work of the novelist Agustina Bessa-Luís. In this case, Oliveira had asked Bessa-Luís for a story for the film. She began writing a novel provisionally titled "Pedra de Toque" (Touchstone) and set in the Convento de Arrábida, a sixteenth-century monastery built on a mountain overlooking the sea near Setúbal, south of Lisbon. Given the time it takes to write a novel and Oliveira's hurry to shoot, he asked her to summarize the story for him. Based on that summary, he wrote the screenplay with no further suggestions from the novelist. He apparently did not even read the work when it appeared in 1994 with the title *As Terras do Risco* (Lands of risk, 1994). Although the point of departure is the same, the narratives thus diverge significantly (Bénard da Costa, "Pedra" 26).

In *The Convent*, perhaps Oliveira's most enigmatic film, Malkovich plays the role of Michael Padovic, an American scholar who goes to Portugal to do research in support of his theory that Shakespeare was a Spaniard of Jewish descent—Jacques Perez—who was forced to leave Spain because of the Inquisition. His wife Hélène (Deneuve) accompanies him on his journey to Arrábida, where Michael believes he may find documents that prove his rather strained hypothesis. The couple, however, is undergoing some kind of marital crisis, as evidenced by Hélène's somewhat sarcastic comment that her husband, who "wants to be immortalized," finds his work more important than her. They sleep in separate rooms, Michael shows indifference to her caress, and, during their second night in the convent, they wage a "war" of slamming doors and the turning on and off of lights.

Like previous films such as *Benilde ou a Virgem-Mãe, O Passado e o Presente,* and *A Divina Comédia,* the action of *The Convent* occurs in a limited space, here largely enclosed by the ancient walls of the monastery, and with a restricted number of characters. When Michael and Hélène arrive at the monastery they are greeted by the guardian, Baltar (Luís Miguel Cintra), then by his assistant, Balthazar (Duarte de Almeida), and the housekeeper, Berta (Heloísa Miranda). Baltar represents a diabolical figure, always dressed in black or black and red, and the other two serve almost as his echoes. Balthazar and Berta are associated visually with the skull of a mountain goat and dramatically with

Catherine Deneuve and John Malkovich in *The Convent* (Cinemateca Portuguesa).

such things as tarot and astrology. While showing them the monastery grounds, Balthazar recoils as he looks at a mask representing the sun in a small chapel. During the first meeting of all five of them, Oliveira films Baltar standing against the backdrop of an inverted pentagram, a traditional symbol of evil. The upturned legs of the pentagram behind his head also associate him with the male deity known as the Horned God. His quarters, and those of Berta, are illuminated by red lights and are filled with objects related to the occult or the demonic.

Baltar is taken with Hélène from the first time he meets her. His ardor intensifies as he lurks in the dark hallways outside her room and witnesses her discord with her husband. Michael, in turn, becomes attracted to Piedade (Leonor Silveira), a beautiful young woman who will serve as his assistant in the monastery's archive. In contrast to the other characters, Piedade is luminous in her light blue clothing, her seeming distance from the conflicts in play, and her dedication, which leads Michael to compare her to Penelope, Odysseus's faithful wife. Her name can be translated as "piety," and she represents purity as, in her words, "the only path to eternal life."

The Convent is filled with references to—and readings from—Goethe's *Faust*. The association of Baltar with Mephistopheles and of Balthazar and Berta with evil or the occult is obvious, indeed explicit, as is the association of Hélène with Helen of Troy and Michael with Faust, particularly because of his quest for knowledge and repeated references to his supposed concern with immortality. Nevertheless, one should be cautious in positing a complete parallel. It is not Michael who makes a pact with Baltar but rather Hélène, whom Balthazar and Berta refer to as a "dangerous" woman. And the roles in the pact may well be reversed. Hélène tells Baltar that she will give in to his desires if he avenges her of wrongs supposedly committed by Piedade, keeping her from falling into Michael's arms.

Although Hélène may seem to be on the side of evil (like Baltar, she often wears black), while Piedade is associated with purity, the film establishes an identification between the two, as if they were two sides of the same being. The morning after the "night of slamming doors," Berta tells Balthazar that Hélène and Piedade are mysterious women and that neither has an astrological sign since they do not fit any astral patterns. Balthazar responds that he thought they were Gemini. Berta does not have enough information about them, although she suspects that to be the case. Everything about them, she says, is enigmatic, and they reveal "a strange superposition of astrological maps." A bit later in the film, when Michael—perhaps sleepwalking—enters Piedade's room and kisses her, both Piedade and Hélène react with pleasure. (We see the kiss, by the way, as shadows on the wall, a phantasmatic representation akin to Oliveira's notion of the cinematic image.) Still later, after Baltar has entered into a pact with Hélène, Michael is seated at his desk in the monastery's archive when the door opens and Piedade appears. She is dressed in black, rather than her usual baby blue, and her hair resembles Hélène's. He looks over to where she had been seated moments before. When he looks back, it is Hélène, not Piedade, who is at the door. This leads Michael to a certain level of understanding, cast in terms of Helen of Troy and the gift of ubiquity that he derives from a passage of *Faust* that Hélène had left open on his desk.

Like *Faust, The Convent* deals with a quest for knowledge, understanding, and perhaps immortality in a world shaped by good and evil. As Oliveira explains, "Since we cannot live our lives without evil, unless we are prepared to renounce mundane interests, a normal life must be no more than one in which the two opposing forces are balanced in a perfect or ideal symbiosis."[25] The film offers multiple images of a statue of a Franciscan monk who apparently attempted this renunciation. Arms outstretched, with a candle in one hand and the handle of a whip in the other, he is blindfolded, his mouth is closed, and there is a keyhole over his heart. The statue rests on a wall outside the passageway into the archive, where, as Baltar says, one can find wisdom comparable to the knowledge of God, which, in Michael's view, is the knowledge of good and evil.

The monastery is a propitious space for this quest, with its cells, chapels, and caves, with multiple references to religious and historical legends, particularly involving the Virgin Mary. Nearby is a Jurassic forest that hides an "abyss of instincts" and a cavern near the ocean that, according to Baltar, is one of the devil's abandoned furnaces. These spaces, plus the numerous mutilated statues Oliveira films, lend the drama a sense of timelessness. Visually, *The Convent* is a film of passageways, beginning from the initial shot, when Michael and Hélène arrive at the monastery gates. Characters constantly pass through doorways and corridors or gaze through openings in walls. Oliveira's camera is frequently placed on the side of the unknown: inside the monastery gates looking out, inside a chapel or cell as the characters look in, and so forth. The film's music, by Stravinsky, Gubaidulina, and Mayazumi, ranges from the eerie and the strident to the somber, and the often dimly lit sets contribute to the reflective, even metaphysical mood that Oliveira evokes.

One cannot, of course, ignore the irony in the film's premise—a search for the "true" identity of Shakespeare—nor its conclusion. After Piedade disappears, lured to the Jurassic forest by Baltar, Michael goes down the mountain to the beach, which is empty except for a rugged fisherman. Suddenly Hélène emerges from the water, walks toward Michael, and puts on a white tunic with gold trim. They walk off down the beach together. A final explanatory note informs us that "[t]he fisherman learned that Hélène and Michael were living happily in Paris and that the professor had given up his research into Jacques Perez in order to study the occult, but not everything he says is to be believed." An appropriate word of caution, I would think.

Party

The satirical *Party*, which was shot on the island of São Miguel in the Azores, features the French actor Michel Piccoli, the Greek actress Irene Pappas, the Oliveira regular Leonor Silveira, and Rogério Samora, who had minor roles in several previous Oliveira films. Based on an original idea by Oliveira, the dialogues were written by Agustina Bessa-Luís, who also recommended the oceanside manor where the director shot the film. Oliveira had originally planned to call the film "A parte da parte perdida no Garden-Party" (The part of the part lost in the garden-party), from Mephistopheles's line in *Faust*, "I'm a part of the Part that first was all, / part of the Darkness that gave birth to Light" (36).

The preliminary title might suggest continuity with *The Convent*, and the two films have a number of things in common, particularly the playing out of a process of estrangement and reconciliation within a relatively restricted space. But *Party* tends much more toward Buñuelian satire than does *The Convent*, and in this sense it recalls *O Passado e o Presente* more than any other Oliveira film. Acknowledging the film's affinities with Buñuel, Emmanuel Dreux has suggested that Oliveira's mise-en-scène in *Party* extracts a "strange alchemy" from the staging of desire or the "ambiguities of its obscure object" (147).

Party brings two couples together on separate occasions five years apart. It alternates conversations among the four of them together with others among two pairs: Leonor and Michel, and Irene and Rogério. Oliveira does not use cross-cutting to give a sense of the simultaneity of the conversations. Rather, he employs a more theatrical structure in which one conversation plays itself out in its entirety, followed by another that took place simultaneously. Like other Oliveira works, *Party* is a "talking picture" in which language has precedence over action.

Nevertheless, the film's setting, a manor overlooking the Atlantic Ocean, is important for understanding its dynamics. Its dialogues include multiple references to elements of nature—water (the sea, rain), wind, fire, the earth (the grassy terrace, but particularly the island's volcanic nature)—all of which find correspondences in the image track. The film's epigraph, superimposed on a black screen and accompanied by the voice of Irene Pappas singing a traditional Greek song, also emphasizes the force of nature: "I have told you that one needs to be careful beside the sea / Beside the raging sea waves will grab you and you will be lost. / If they grab me, where will they take me? / To the depths of the sea. / I will make a boat of my body and oars of my hands."

At the same time, inside the house Oliveira's camera often focuses on fixtures such as statuettes and the imposing fireplace mantle, said to have been made by one of Michaelangelo's disciples, offering a sense of relative permanence. The film's two main spaces—the house and its grounds, including a nearby beach—on one level represent the dichotomy between nature and artifice, although in reality the two are intertwined. They are metaphorical expressions of the tension between nature (or instinct) and culture (or the sublimation of those instincts) in human, and particularly amorous, relationships. As Emmanuel Dreux has observed, *Party* oscillates between "the comedy of (sexual) desire and the tragedy of (amorous) desire" (147).

Party is divided into two parts, each of which corresponds to one of the two spaces described above. In the first, Leonor and Rogério—all of the characters have the same names as the actors who play them—have been married for ten years. As the film opens, Leonor is alone on the grassy terrace overlooking the sea, a shot that associates her with nature.

Rogério Samora, Leonor Silveira,
Michel Piccoli, and Irene Pappas in *Party*
(Cinemateca Portuguesa).

Her husband is inside, looking down at Leonor through a window. He is
thus associated with artifice or convention. Leonor has decided to throw
a garden party, although in reality she thinks the idea of such events is old
hat. She even facetiously suggests that the two of them flee just as their
guests begin to arrive. Among them are the entrepreneur and former
actress Irene and her lover, the philanderer and gambler Michel. The
four of them engage in rather cynical and often sarcastic banter about
life, love, sex, and relationships.

Leonor and Michel distance themselves from the rest of the group,
first on the grassy terrace, then on the beach below, filled with black
volcanic rocks. Their sometimes flirtatious dialogue soon turns to their
perceptions of each other. Michel says that Leonor is a "good girl," but
not an interesting woman like Irene. She responds that all of the men
she has known have wanted to marry her, which proves that he is right.
Leonor sees Michel as a "general in the war of the sexes," compared to
whom her husband is a mere recruit. As their suggestive conversation
progresses, Michel, an incorrigible Don Juan, declares his fascination
with and passion for Leonor, which is "like a bolt of lightning that comes

from the sea and breaks him into pieces." Leonor says that he startles her and that they should go back to the party.

Meanwhile, Irene and Rogério engage in their own conversation about love and relationships while seated at a table near the other guests (who have no speaking roles). When Irene asks if he loves his wife, Rogério responds, "Not exactly," and he confesses that Leonor has made it clear that she likes him but does not love him. Leonor and Michel return, and the four continue their conversation together. In many ways, Leonor's conversation with Michel on the beach is the fulcrum of the film. At one point, Michel provocatively says that he and Leonor had made love on the beach, leading Rogério to threaten to make him leave. Their conversation is interrupted by a storm blowing in, which makes all the guests run inside, ending the first part.

The film's second part takes place in the same manor five years later, when Irene and Miguel again visit Leonor and Rogério. It opens with a Buñuelesque touch, as the four of them are seated around a long dinner table with no food. Between Leonor and Rogério, impeding their view of each other, are two statues of angels holding small lampposts. To see each other, they have to lean to the right or the left. Between Irene and Miguel is a large, artificial barricuda. For them to see each other, they have to stretch their necks to look over it, or put their heads on the table to look under it.

After a brief initial conversation between the four of them that ranges from witty to ironic to sarcastic, Irene and Rogério move over by the fireplace, while Leonor and Michel stay near the table. With others listening in, Leonor tells Michel that even though she doesn't love him, she has not been able to get him out of her mind since their conversation on the beach five years earlier, and she will go away with him if he wants. He responds that he has come to take her away. They soon exit the room, leaving Irene and Rogério alone to talk about women, the tedium of relationships, and the possibility of betrayal. Rogério says that his wife may give a man a place at the table and in bed, but not in her heart, as if it were a matter of "renting" the space.

In the end, Leonor and Michel return, telling the others that they are going to leave together. Irene tells them that there is always room for one more in the car, and in bed. Outside the house, Irene and Michel pace back and forth in different directions, showing their discomfort with the situation that has emerged. Leonor comes out with her suitcase, and Michel stops his pacing to talk to her. Irene stalks off to the car and starts honking. Leonor drops her suitcase to the ground, and Michel joins Irene in the car, which speeds off. Rogério comes to the door and tells Leonor that she should have gone with them, since he is totally broke. Leonor tells him that that is the most exciting thing he has said today. When Rogério says that he doesn't know if they can forget what has happened, Leonor responds that she is too young to remember it. They go inside together when it starts to pour down rain. The film ends with a slapstick scene in which Rogério runs back out to get Leonor's suitcase. He slips and falls on the wet pavement, then the bag opens and clothes fall out when he tries to pick it up. He has trouble getting in the door because of the umbrella, but eventually he does, and he closes it behind him, ending the film. *Party* is not one of Oliveira's greatest films, but it represents an accessible example of some of the cinematic techniques and strategies that he had been developing for many years. In his next film, he would return to the more daring aesthetic that characterizes many of his earlier works.

Voyages

In *Viagem ao Princípio do Mundo* (Voyage to the beginning of the world; 1997), an aging film director named Manoel, played by Marcello Mastroianni (1924–96) in his final screen role, and three actors travel across northern Portugal so that Afonso (Jean-Yves Gautier)—a French actor of Portuguese descent—can visit places his father told him about but that he himself has never seen. In particular, he wants to meet his father's sister, Maria Afonso (Isabel de Castro), who still lives in Lugar do Teso, near Castro Laboreiro in the extreme north of the country. Accompanying Manoel and Afonso are Judite (Leonor Silveira) and Duarte (Diogo Dória). Along the way, Manoel intends to revisit some of the places of his youth. Manoel de Oliveira himself is the driver. Although he does not appear frequently, and he does not speak, his appearances are sufficient for the spectator to draw the appropriate connection between him and his alter ego, the fictional director played by Mastroianni. They have the same first name, they wear similar floppy brimmed hats, and at some points the mise-en-scène aligns them so that it seems as if one is a visual echo of the other.[26]

The journey thus develops two distinct but closely related dramatic lines. The first, which goes from the beginning of the film until the group's arrival in Lugar do Teso, involves Manoel's nostalgic return, as along the way he reminisces about the people and places of his youth: the Jesuit boarding school across the river from Caminha, the statue of Pedro Macau, and the Grand Hotel de Pezo, where Manoel would go with his brothers when he was an adolescent. The second part, which takes place largely in Lugar do Teso, focuses not on physical travel but on the (re)establishment of family ties and the transformation of identity. Afonso's journey is not precisely the same as Manoel's, even though they are on the road together. Whereas Manoel's trip is characterized by return, on the one hand, and distance and impossibility, on the other hand, Afonso's is one of discovery, increasing proximity, and hopeful possibility. Their journey traverses multiple personal and national temporalities in a sort of metaphorical time travel to a time of identity formation, seen in retrospective and prospective terms. It is a film of return, reminiscence, and *le temps perdu* as the director moves inexorably toward the end of his life. At the same time, it is a film of discovery, hope, and transformation, as one of the actors connects with his roots and begins to understand his own identity in a way that he never had before.

The film is based loosely on true stories: Manoel de Oliveira's youth in northern Portugal and the experience of the actor Yves Afonso, the son of a Portuguese emigrant to France who traveled to Portugal in 1987 to participate in a Franco-Portuguese film production.[27] A strikingly profound variation on the road movie, *Voyage to the Beginning of the World* focuses on the interactions among the four characters and on questions of memory, aging, time, and identity. Sequences frequently take place within the confined space of the car, and when they do stop along the way, the emphasis is on dialogue—mostly in French—rather than action.

Although Oliveira's camera is normally static, the film is not. Movement takes multiple forms in *Voyage:* shots from a fixed camera looking out the back window of the moving car, the movement of objects or people in the frame, cuts from one shot to another, and, perhaps most importantly, the movement of language and ideas. The film is replete with historical and literary references, providing a historical density that allows it to go beyond the existential issues confronting the characters to a broader focus on questions involving language and the nation.

Voyage to the Beginning of the World opens with a recurring visual motif: a shot looking out from the back window of the car. In this case, the shot—a dizzying seventy-one seconds—focuses on the highway. No scenery, just the gray pavement divided by single or double white stripes, with an occasional arrow indicating a turn lane, and the wheels of other cars going in the other direction. Similar shots provide transitions between the film's narrative blocks, as the car moves forward and the highway and countryside recede. Accompanied by the atonal music of Emmanuel Nunes (b. 1941), these transitions provide a distancing effect, as if the automobile and its passengers are in fact traveling into the past.

With the camera still focused on the road, the initial dialogue begins in medias res, presenting some of the film's major themes: age and aging,

Marcello Mastroianni in *Voyage to the Beginning of the World* (Cinemateca Portuguesa).

death, memory, *saudade*, atavism, and identity. The dialogue foregrounds the question of age, as Judite and Manoel talk about age differences. Their divergent attitudes concerning the matter reflect their respective ages. Manoel insists on the impact of aging because he experiences it daily. He walks with a cane, he feels the deterioration of the body, even if his mind remains strong, and he knows that death is not far away. Despite the fact that he is a respected film director ("a respected *old* director," he says), he also knows that age and illness keep people apart and that the young prefer the company of the young, leaving the old behind. The question of age and death is made more poignant by the fact that Mastroianni died not long after filming *Voyage to the Beginning of the World,* which is dedicated to him.

Judite attempts to dismiss the issue of age, perhaps because it doesn't yet affect her directly. Young, intelligent, and beautiful, she can look optimistically toward the future, and she therefore has the freedom to be ironic, sarcastic, and even sexually suggestive, as well as to make light of Manoel's concerns. Even her clothes—a white and blue outfit with a sailor's motif—express a rather ironic perspective on the journey. Her mildly and playfully seductive attitude leads Duarte, who often provides his companions with the historical or cultural context of what they are seeing or saying, to compare her somewhat hyperbolically to the biblical Judith, who charmed and murdered the Assyrian general Holofernes.

Closely related to age is the question of memory. Manoel's return to places he had known in the past is impossible, and not only because of the inexistence of "real" time travel. Things and places have changed or are out of reach. The boarding school he attended is on the far side of the river, and it can be seen clearly only with binoculars. The statue of Pedro Macau is not where he remembers it being, and it has lost an arm to vandals. The Grand Hotel in Pezo, where he vacationed as an adolescent, is now a crumbling ruin.

The first stop along the road is in Caminha, across the Minho River from the Spanish city of La Guardia, where Mastroianni's Manoel—and Manoel de Oliveira—studied in a Jesuit boarding school at the age of ten or eleven. Reminiscing about certain formative moments of his past, Manoel recalls the harsh conditions of the school, the discipline and punishment to which he and the other students were subjected, sin or sinful thoughts, and confession. As the camera accompanies a crew team rowing smoothly across the water, Manoel talks about the fear he felt when he had to cross the river in a small boat to return home for the holidays. The waves made them feel as if they were at sea, and he was afraid of drowning. The boatman, however, was calm. In Manoel's words, as rendered by the English subtitles, he was "small and tough, thin and dry," but he seemed like a giant.

In addition to personal reminiscences about the past, this initial sequence also includes significant historical resonances. In the course of the conversation, references are made to the Portuguese monarchy, the Republic, the expulsion of Jesuits in 1910, and, implicitly, Portugal's relations with Spain. It is no coincidence that one of the travelers is named Duarte, perhaps after Portugal's philosopher-king who ruled from 1433–38 and supported the expeditions of his brother, Prince Henry the Navigator (1394–1460), who, acting like a human giant, led the ships of a "small and tough, thin and dry" country on some of the most important navigations of European history.

As they continue on their journey, Manoel remembers a statue he once saw along the road when traveling with his father and brothers. The statue is of a figure called Pedro Macau, a man on one knee supporting a huge log on his shoulders. The statue is not precisely where Manoel remembers it to have been, and it has changed: it has lost an arm, and the trellis that once existed on top of the log is no longer there. A local woman tells them a poem about Pedro Macau, who is in perpetual "exile" because he cannot put the log down. Critics tend to see the statue as a symbol of the human condition, human suffering, or the inability to escape one's past or destiny. Stephen Holden, however, interprets it as a "symbol of the aged director himself carrying on in a world that barely seems to notice" ("'Voyage'").

The film's most poignant sequence takes place outside what is left of the Grande Hotel de Pezo. As they drive through Pezo toward the hotel, Manoel's facial expression reveals an air of restrained excitement, but when the car moves through its gates the image becomes darker, presumably because the car is driving under trees. The shift from light to dark, however, is metaphorical, anticipating the sequence that is about to begin and expressing the long but inexorable transition from youth to old age.

When the car stops and the passengers exit, the camera is at a distance. As the group begins to move away from the car, Emmanuel Nunes's plaintive piano accompanies the scene. The camera tracks as they walk slowly across the shaded grounds, with Oliveira hovering silently in the background, then it travels, in a low-angle shot, along the hotel's decaying walls, before Manoel walks off by himself. He sees a flower on the branch of a small tree, and he tries but is unable to reach it. A well-worn metaphor for youth, his inability to reach the flower visually represents the impossibility of return. When he walks back to his traveling companion, he appears even frailer than before, saying simply, "Que désolation," referring to the hotel ruins and to himself, but also to the modern world, with its destructive tendencies.

Afonso's story begins in earnest only after the group leaves Pezo, where he tells Manoel that the past they have been discussing was his (Manoel's) and that it has nothing to do with him, since it is not his father's past. Although Afonso tells his companions his father's story—his departure from Portugal, his arrest in Spain, his escape to France, his hardship and successes, his early death—the narrative shift takes place only after the group stops at a bridge between Castro Laboreiro and Lugar do Teso. In this sequence, not a word is spoken. After they get out of the car, Manoel and his driver stand side by side—for the first time in the film—on the bridge by which they stopped, while Afonso, Duarte, and Judite walk to a much older, more primitive bridge a few yards away. The sequence's final shot—looking through the old bridge to the more modern one—is again metaphorical, representing not only transition but also coexistent or superimposed temporalities.

Lugar do Teso is an extremely isolated village that seems to have stopped in time. Indeed, within the context of the film, it is the "beginning of the world." There, Afonso and his fellow travelers meet his aunt, Maria Afonso, who, according to Stéphane Bouquet, is a veritable phantasm, "carrying with her the mystery of the origins" (72). Toughened by a hard life, she seems to belong to an earlier, almost premodern age, at the beginning of the nation and the inception of the family. One should remember that the word *princípio* in Portuguese has at least two meanings: "beginning" and "principle." Maria Afonso represents both the beginning and the fundamental or underlying principle of the world through and to which Afonso and the others travel.

Their initial encounter takes place in the house of Maria Afonso's daughter-in-law, Cristine (Cécile Sanz de Alba), a young French woman who married Maria Afonso's son (Afonso's cousin). The encounter is marked by suspicion and difficulty in communication, since Afonso does not speak Portuguese, and Maria Afonso repeatedly asks, "Por que não fala nossa fala?" (Why doesn't he speak our language?). They can only communicate indirectly and imperfectly through translation. Finally, unable to convince her that he is in fact her nephew, Afonso stands, takes off his coat, walks over to his aunt, asks her to put her hand on his arm, and tells her that what matters is blood, not language, and that they have the same blood in their veins.

The following sequence takes us to the origins of the Portuguese nation, to the beginning and principle of the world. Afonso asks to go to the cemetery to see where his ancestors are buried. Maria Afonso wants to change clothes before she goes, so the group goes up the hill to her house. As they walk, Duarte asks José, Maria Afonso's husband, why all of the mailboxes have the name Afonso on them. He replies that they are all descendents of Afonso Henriques, Portugal's founder. In the ensuing conversation, which takes place in a dark house without electricity, Maria Afonso and José recognize that when they die, there will be nothing left, since the young people have left and are not interested in the kind of life they lead.

Language, ancestry, and nation are traditionally seen as the pillars of identity. But are things really that simple? Despite Afonso's successful encounter with his aunt, *Voyage to the Beginning of the World* problematizes the question of identity, particularly through a number of references to contemporaneous wars in Bosnia and Croatia, where conflicts generated by deep-seated ethnic identities resulted in hundreds of thousands of deaths and the horrendous resurgence of ethnic cleansing. Atavism can clearly have a positive side, as with Afonso's journey to his roots, but it can also be much, much darker. In the film's initial sequence, Manoel's reference to Sarajevo leads Duarte, who is looking directly into the camera, to say simply, "Apocalypse now." Later, when contemplating the ruins of the Grande Hotel do Pezo and discussing the perhaps fatal illness of the modern world, Duarte compares the situation to "Sarajevo without the bullets." Even Maria Afonso, who reveals an abiding concern with the negative impact of war, refers to the situation in Croatia.

Jonathan Romney suggests that *Voyage to the Beginning of the World* is "an entirely unsentimental enquiry into endangered national identity, by a director who has made a specialty of being linguistically and culturally polyglot. [It] has mainly French dialogue, with most of the Portuguese translated back into French for Afonso's benefit" (34). In this sense, the historical subtext that runs throughout the film—with references to events ranging from the nation's founding to the European Union—becomes even more significant, especially when seen in relation to comments, made at certain moments of the film, that Portuguese is not important in France and that "nobody cares about us," or references, starting with Afonso's father, to emigration to other countries.

Although it raises all of these issues, at least tangentially, *Voyage to the Beginning of the World* is not a political film per se. It focuses on the personal and on existential issues related to the passing of time, aging, and death. Manoel's journey to the beginning of the world is a journey toward death, a fact made painfully clear in one of the final sequences in the film, which takes place in a cemetery. As Afonso and his aunt Maria Afonso kneel together, their hands clasped, Manoel walks off by himself. In a long shot, the camera focuses on him surrounded by gravestones. As he slowly walks offscreen, all that is left on screen are the gravestones. Oliveira's film, however, does not end on this somber note. Rather, it recognizes death as the last act of life, which is characterized by multiple and constant transformations and modulations around a core whose roots are deeper than one might realize.

Inquietude

In the episodic *Inquietude* (Disquiet; 1998), which Jonathan Rosenbaum chose as one of the best movies of 1998, Oliveira weaves together three stories, all of which are drawn from literary works. The first episode, based on Helder Prista Monteiro's one-act play *Os Imortais* (The immortals; 1968), deals with a ninety-plus-year-old man who, upset about his physical and social decrepitude, urges his son to assure his own immortality by killing himself. The second, drawn from António Patrício's short story "Suzy" (ca. 1910) and set in Porto in the 1930s, focuses on a dandy's love for an elegant but ultimately unattainable cocotte. The final episode, based on Agustina Bessa-Luís's fable *A Mãe de um Rio* (The mother of a river; 1971), deals with a young girl from a small rural hamlet who seeks the "mother of the waters" to escape the dullness and oppressiveness of her life.

Oliveira melds the three seemingly unrelated episodes through narrative and cinematic sleight of hand. The first episode is based on a play, but he does not explicitly film it as such, although its framing, decor, and Prista Monteiro's dialogue might seem theatrical. The camera, however, roams through three rooms of an urban apartment, two shots occur in the apartment below, and the film includes an external sequence. It thus comes as a bit of a surprise when a curtain drops at the end and we realize that we have been watching a play. The main characters of the second episode—two unnamed men and two cocottes—are in the audience, and the film picks up their story. As they leave the theater, the two men encounter Suzy and her friend Gabi d'Anjou. After Suzy's unseen death near the end of this episode, the despondent lover's friend tells him the story of the mythical Mother of the River to console him. The three episodes, although quite different in style, thus become one, since the first and the third are in effect narratives—one theatrical, the other oral—embedded in the second.

The episodes are structurally linked, and they are also thematically related in that they all deal with disquieting questions related to life, death, love, and immortality. In the first episode, old age represents the destruction of one's identity, which has been constructed over time and legitimated through social and professional recognition. The only way to maintain that identity and assure immortality, according to the somewhat demented father, is to die at the height of one's fame and glory. The second focuses on the transitory nature of existence and the impossibility of enduring love in certain circumstances, while at the same time praising life as movement and creativity. The third, shifting to the level of myth, offers a reflection on immortality and freedom from societal constraints.

The initial episode opens with a sequence shot of the elderly father (José Pinto) in his disheveled study. Clearly perturbed, he paces around the room, accompanied on the soundtrack by a frantic piano concerto. Finally, he walks through the curtains covering a doorway, across a room, and into another room where his son (Luís Miguel Cintra), himself elderly, is working at his desk. The father utters the words, "Kill yourself!" before going back to his own study. The son, perplexed, looks up at the art nouveau statuettes of a young man and a young woman on his desk—which Oliveira's camera captures in close-ups—before getting up to go speak with his father.

If, in *Voyage to the Beginning of the World,* Oliveira offers a poignant view of aging, in the initial episode of *Inquietude* his take is much more humorous, although the humor is decidedly dark. The father sees old age as a monstrosity. He repeatedly tells his son that "they" have killed him, or at least half of him, and the remaining half is a monster whom nobody remembers and who is left to deal with his medication, his forgetfulness, and his physical decay. He ties a handkerchief around his wrist so he will remember that he exists. His son tries to reason with him, to no avail.

Ruy Gardnier has noted that the father and son are "men of science," professionals "dedicated to freezing time and extracting universal constants" ("Inquietude"). The only sign of vitality in the apartment is a photograph of a woman (Isabel Ruth) who was apparently the best student of both father and son. To attempt to convince his father that he is wrong about the idea of attaining immortality through suicide, the son organizes a picnic with the woman. The picnic sequence, which recalls Édouard Manet's *Le Déjeuner sur l'herbe* in its composition, opens with a close shot of a record revolving on a gramophone, followed by a low-angle shot of the woman turning in circles and looking at the trees above. The camera then makes an additional circular movement as it focuses on the trees before the woman begins dancing on the grass in the mode of a silent film. The three circular movements emphasize the cyclical nature of life, which the father wants to cut short, at least for his son, as a means of gaining eternal life through the prestige of his name and theories. As Gardnier puts it, "[W]omen have a primordial role in *Inquietude:* they reveal that the sweetness of life resides in gestures. They desire action, whereas men prefer things as they are; they want life, while men struggle for eternity" ("Inquietude").

The episode ends back in the apartment. Unable to convince his son to kill himself, the father asks him to at least fix the curtain. The son climbs onto a chair to do so, and the father pushes him out the window. Again evoking silent cinema, the film cuts to the apartment below, where we see the son hanging from the curtain outside the window before falling to his death. The father initially thinks that he has been successful,

The picnic in *Inquietude* (Madragoa Filmes). |

and if his son is now immortal, then he is free from any guilt for having killed him. He soon realizes, however, that without his son he has lost the other half of himself, and he too jumps to his death.

The second episode deals with a man's relationship with Suzy (Leonor Silveira), a cocotte who frequents Porto's high society. The love-struck man (Diogo Dória) is inconsolable. Although he can have Suzy's body, he cannot control her or reach her in any deeper sense. And yet he continually repeats the words "poor Suzy," perhaps because of an underlying condescension because she does not fit his bourgeois ideal of eternal love. As for Suzy, everything is "just a detail." Love and happiness seem to be ephemeral. This is yet another twist on Oliveira's oft explored them of unfulfilled love.

Midway in the episode is a sequence that perhaps only Manoel de Oliveira could include. It takes place in a nightclub, and it opens with a man's hands playing a tango on a piano. Couples and groups are seated at tables, while a single elegant couple dances the tango across the floor. The dancers in question are Manoel de Oliveira and his wife, Isabel, as if a comment on immortality and his own longevity. In its brief introduction to a series of reviews of *Inquietude*, the editors of *Cahiers du Cinéma* write the following: "A filmmaker who, in the middle of his film, suddenly passes by dancing a subtle tango is a filmmaker who can permit himself anything. He is sovereign, free, unique, perched high on a tightrope that no one else can reach, defying the laws of gravity and above all the rules of cinematic decorum and commerce. *Inquietude* is the film that affirms his liberty, his fantasy, his melancholy, and his supremacy. For in this film Manoel de Oliveira totally merges his stature as a man and his prestige as an auteur. In it he delicately imposes his signature: the ironic, changing, cultivated manner of an immense cinéaste" ("Oliveira le funambule"). Very well said.

The final episode of *Inquietude,* told partially in voiceover by the inconsolable lover's friend, deals with Fisalina (Leonor Baldaque), a young woman "given to dreams and inexplicable sadness" who is unhappy in her small village with its stone walls, its narrow stone streets, and its small life and with her uninspiring boyfriend. She wants something different, to be with people who pronounce unknown words. Because of her unsatisfactory situation, she seeks the wisdom of the Mother of the River (Irene Pappas). The first time we see the Mother of the River, she is singing a traditional Greek song while brushing her long black hair. In a voiceover, she speaks of transformation, memory, and oblivion, saying that she is no longer able to sing as when she was younger and that her feet no longer feel the earth's murmur. The people of the village have forgotten her, and she does not recognize the new generations of children, who all seem to be the same.

When Fisalina goes to her cabin in the woods, the Mother of the River reads to her about the creation of the world from Hesiod's *Theogony.* She tells Fisalina that she had read in Greek as they pronounce it today, since Ancient Greek has been forgotten. Their dialogue takes place without translation in two languages, Greek and Portuguese, and they have no problem understanding each other.[28] The use of Greek and the reading from Hesiod associate the Mother of the River with the origins of the world and, more specifically, with the origins of Western civilization, and her golden fingertips associate her with nature.

Fisalina tells the Mother of the River that she feels entrapped in her village; the streets have grown like stone wheat, and the walls have closed in on her. She wants freedom and movement. She pleads, "Curse me, but let me be free." The Mother of the River responds: "The sun is made of fire and salt. . . . Whoever is free has doused the fire and melted the salt and will have no place in matter." She then takes Fisalina into a cavern illuminated by candles. Oliveira's camera anticipates them with a splendid backwards traveling shot. When the Mother of the River asks Fisalina to look down, water emerges from the ground below. Fisalina turns around, but the Mother of the River has gone.

The girl goes back to her village, and one night while she is seated at her desk writing, she notices that her fingertips have become golden. She has taken on the Mother of the River's characteristics, and she is enchanted by the transformation. She tries to hide her fingers from her family—even wearing a glove at dinner—but one night, during a religious procession, someone sees her fingers, and she is chased out of town, with the women running behind her yelling "witch!" Fisalina is at last free, as she replaces the Mother of the River, but her freedom comes at the cost of withdrawing from the social world and being condemned to a thousand years of solitude in communion with nature.

As we have seen in previous films, love in Oliveira is a perhaps unattainable ideal, as is complete freedom. The same may be said for happiness and the desire for immortality, which comes only in death or in isolation from the social world, or in the movement of a nonagenarian dancing the tango across a movie screen.

La Lettre

After *Inquietude,* Oliveira continued to pursue his wide-ranging literary interests with *La Lettre* (The letter; 1999), a free adaptation of Madame de Lafayette's classic novel, *The Princess of Clèves* (1678). *La Lettre* can best be understood by relating it to concerns Oliveira first explored in his tetralogy of frustrated love and in subsequent films such as *Le Soulier de satin* and *Abraham's Valley.* According to Oliveira, the idea of filming the novel dates from the time he was shooting *Amor de Perdição,* when he met and became friends with Jacques Parsi, his close collaborator and translator. Given Oliveira's interest in the theme of frustrated love, Parsi recommended that he consider adapting Stendahl's *The Charterhouse of Parma,* Claudel's *Le Soulier de satin,* and Madame de Lafayette's novel, none of which the director had read at the time. Oliveira directed *Le Soulier de satin* in 1985, but he felt that adapting Stendahl's novel would be too complicated, so the idea never matured.[29] It took him more than twenty years to fulfill his ambition of filming *The Princess of Clèves. La Lettre,* which won a Jury Award in the 1999 Cannes Film Festival, has more in common with earlier films than it does with some of the other films he made in the 1990s.

Oliveira updates Lafayette's late seventeenth-century amorous tale to contemporary Paris and the nobility into the Parisian upper class. He casts Chiara Mastroianni (the daughter of Marcello Mastroianni and Catherine Deneuve) in the role of Catherine de Clèves, and he replaces the dashing Duke of Nemours with the somewhat eccentric Portuguese rock star Pedro Abrunhosa, who plays himself. Like the novel on which it is based, *La Lettre* deals with a young woman (Mademoiselle de Chartres/Madame de Clèves) who marries a man she does not love (Jacques de Clèves, played by Antoine Chappey) and then falls in love with another man (Abrunhosa). Out of respect and fidelity to her husband, and because of her own moral code of behavior, she refuses to act on that love, although she confesses it to her husband, thus contributing to his illness and death. Even after she is widowed and thus free, Madame de Clèves will not pursue her love for Abrunhosa, preferring instead to disappear from view. Oliveira reduces the novel to this dramatic core and adds important elements: Abrunhosa's concerts, which open and close the film; Madame de Clèves's confessional conversations with a childhood friend who has become a nun (played by Leonor Silveira), and the letter from Madame de Clèves to the nun, who reads it aloud in one of the film's final sequences.

Numerous critics have pointed out the anachronism inherent in Oliveira's strategy, for the moral strictures guiding the heroine's behavior in the novel hardly apply to late twentieth-century Paris. Stephen Holden suggests that Catherine de Clèves's "questions about loyalty, virtue, honor and trust . . . may have been vital issues in Roman Catholic France three centuries ago but . . . today hardly anybody anywhere bothers to ask [them]" ("'Letter'"). Holden notes, however, that what Oliveira offers in *La Lettre* is not a realistic love story but rather a "raw spiritual allegory of the war between the flesh and spirit." Oliveira's characters themselves foreground the anachronism. Madame de Clèves recognizes that no one cares about reputation today and that few of her friends share her values. Beyond such comments, Oliveira's camera frequently focuses on objects such as statues in the Jardin de Luxembourg that give a sense of permanence, even while action may be fleeting.

Rather than attempting to force *La Lettre* into an entirely verisimilar

Pedro Abrunhosa and Manoel de Oliveira during the shooting of *La Lettre* (Madragoa Filmes).

mode, it is more productively seen in relation to Oliveira's earlier explorations of unfulfilled love. Constrained by society, family, or their own obsessions, his characters sacrifice the real possibility of love in the name of a distant and ultimately unattainable ideal. Somewhat like Prouhèze in *Le Soulier de satin,* Madame de Clèves renounces any possibility of physical love and sublimates her desire before disappearing and going to Africa. She does so in part because of a perhaps anachronistic view of morality inculcated by her mother ("morality is morality," her mother tells a friend). But she also does so because of the fear that involvement or marriage to Abrunhosa could result in his breaking the "enchantment of impossible love." Oliveira seems to be suggesting in this and earlier films that pure love can only exist as an ideal, but not in a physical, corporeal, or "real" sense.

In earlier films, such as *Amor de Perdição* and *Francisca,* the pursuit of pure love led to death. Madame de Clèves's refusal, in contrast, leads her to the world outside, the world of human pain and suffering. In her final discussion at the convent, her friend tells her that her attitude of renunciation is nonsensical and that she might as well become a nun. Madame de Clèves responds that she does not have the calling. She finds a different calling, however, in Africa, where she goes almost by chance and whence she writes the letter that gives the film its title. Immediately before the film's final shot, of an Abrunhosa concert in which he sings a song—"Será" (Could it be?)—is a beautiful sequence that takes place in the convent. In the first two shots, the nun (played by Leonor Silveira) reads, first in a medium-shot, then in close-up, a letter that Madame de Clèves has written from Africa. She has gone there almost by chance after having met a group of young nuns who were departing to work with refugees in an unnamed country torn by civil war. She describes the refugees' suffering, as well as the hardship borne by the nuns, who nevertheless always seem to be able to smile. She wonders how men, blinded by greed, can "close their eyes to everything for their own lust for power," ignoring the innocent victims left in their wake. She says that the situation makes her want to flee but that her admiration for the nuns' determination makes her stay.

Ruy Gardnier has perceptively noted that Madame de Clèves's experience in Africa, where she often has little to eat, represents a form of sublimation in which the body's suffering functions as a path to overcome the love she feels for Abrunhosa ("Carta"). That is no doubt true, but it may be more complex than that because of the historical associations Oliveira makes. Some of Madame de Clèves's confessions to her religious friend take place in a room in the convent dominated by a large portrait of Mother Angelique Arnaud, who introduced Jansenism to the Port-Royal Abbey and who denied humanity's freedom in the name of a belief in absolute predestination. The film thus establishes a correlation between the nuns' calling and Madame de Clèves's option to depart for Africa in terms of the impossibility of freedom to find love with Abrunhosa or anyone else.

As in other films, Oliveira foregrounds questions of representation and performance in *La Lettre*. The film opens with a shot of a drum set on a dark stage. The applause of an unseen audience fills the soundtrack. The lights come partially up, and a lone saxophonist enters the stage, playing for the audience and the camera. The second shot is of Pedro Abrunhosa sitting before a mirror. When told that it is almost time for him to go on stage, he stands up, puts on his coat, taps his heart with his fist, and walks out the door. The camera remains focused on the mirror, even as the performance begins offscreen. These two long takes—a combined three minutes and twenty-four seconds with a static camera—are vintage Oliveira (with the obvious exception of the music, which is much more contemporary than that which he normally uses). *La Lettre* also closes with a performance by Abrunhosa. He sings the song "Será," which he wrote especially for the film. The song, which serves as a kind of metacommentary and coda, speculates about choices and possibilities.[30]

Palavra e Utopia

In preparing *Non ou a Vã Glória de Mandar*, Oliveira used numerous historical and literary documents, including a sermon from the Jesuit priest António Vieira (1608–97). Ten years later, he would again turn to Vieira in *Palavra e Utopia* (Word and Utopia; 2000). Here, though, Vieira is the film's central focus. Structured largely from letters and sermons written between 1626 and 1695, *Palavra e Utopia* follows Vieira's trajectory from the time he studied in a Jesuit seminary in Salvador, Bahia, until his death in that same city at the age of eighty-nine. The documents incorporated into the film do not always coincide historically with events depicted, and they do not provide a global explanation of his work, but they do give a sense of Vieira's religious and social concerns at different moments of his career. Oliveira uses three actors to represent different phases of Vieira's life—Ricardo Trepa as the young Vieira, Luís Miguel Cintra as the mature Jesuit, and the Brazilian Lima Duarte as the elderly priest—and he provides dates, either in intertitles or orally, for most of the moments presented. To enhance fidelity to his subject, he filmed in the locations in Portugal, Brazil, and Rome where Vieira preached or where his prosecution by the Portuguese Inquisition took place. The film is not, however, a historical biography in any traditional sense of the term.

As indicated by the film's title, Oliveira's focus is more on Vieira's language and ideas than on the events of his life. In a film in which the camera is largely static, motion involves the movement of language more than the movement of images. Echoing Oliveira's view of the importance of language in cinema, Carlos Alberto Mattos suggests that "Vieira's sermons, letters, and reflections are 'actions' that are just as vertiginous as those of a film by John Woo, only they are restricted to the realm of thought. . . . It suffices to give in to the enchantment of

the discourse, the oral 'scenography' of the film's baroque Portuguese
. . . to understand that this is one of the most rapid and lively films in
recent years." Spectators who are reluctant to succumb to the enchantment of the baroque Portuguese discourse, or who don't understand
the language, may find it one of Oliveira's most difficult films.

Palavra e Utopia opens with another of Oliveira's long tracking shots,
this time a low-angle of trees framed against the sky, accompanied by the
sounds of Carlos Paredes's Portuguese guitar. In dramatic terms, its first
sequence is set in 1663, when Vieira appeared before a tribunal of the
Inquisition. In his response to questions, he provides brief background
information about his birth, travel to Brazil, and education. This is one
of the film's few didactic moments. He says that he does not know why
he was called before the Inquisition. He is forced to kneel and pray. A
nondiegetic indigenous chant begins to be heard, and the film cuts to
Brazil many years earlier, initially with a shot of Amerindians dancing
in a circle and chanting. The first part of the film thus takes place as
a flashback from the priest's encounter with the Inquisition, no doubt
with the intention of showing how he came to be seen as heretical.

The film then shows Vieira as a young seminarian (Trepa), defending
indigenous peoples, their land, and the Tupy language in a conversation with fellow students. Subsequent sequences with the young Vieira
involve the Dutch invasion of Salvador (1624), a sermon in which he
contrasts the privilege of whites with the suffering of slaves, and a famous
1649 sermon "against the arms of Holland," in which he asks for divine
assistance against the Dutch invaders. The film's portrait of the young
Vieira is one of a man who is passionate about his defense of the indigenous peoples he wants to catechize for the Catholic church as well as
his attempts to alleviate the suffering of African slaves by convincing
them and their owners that they are sons and daughters of the same
Adam and Eve.

This initial segment, which covers some twenty years of Vieira's life
but less than fifteen minutes of the film, also reveals some of Oliveira's
aesthetic strategies. For example, an intertitle superimposed on an artistic representation of the Portuguese city of Coimbra situates Vieira's
appearance before the Inquisition geographically and chronologically.
Similar illustrations, with or without dates, represent São Luiz, Lisbon,
and Rome. Nondiegetic sound often anticipates a sequence, as with

the Amerindian chant mentioned above, or when a sermon begins as an offscreen voiceover during a shot of slaves singing and dancing and then continues diegetically as the film cuts to inside a chapel where Vieira is preaching. At times the voiceover describes what we see on screen, as when Vieira's 1626 "Carta Ânua" (Annual letter) describes the brutality of the Dutch invasion, which Oliveira portrays visually by showing a group of Dutch soldiers invading a church and wounding a priest, intercut with shots of him reading the letter at his desk. Indeed, throughout the film numerous sequences show Vieira reading a letter he has written, reading (at a slower pace) as he writes, or dictating a letter to his assistant. Oliveira sometimes marks Vieira's trans-Atlantic voyages with shots of the ocean, at times accompanied by a voiceover of a passage from a sermon or an explanatory title.

The mature phase of Vieira (Luís Miguel Cintra) follows his life from the early 1640s until the mid-1670s and incorporates moments that occurred in Maranhão, the Azores, Lisbon, Coimbra, and Rome. After Portugal's King John IV freed Portugal from Spanish rule in 1640, Vieira returned to Lisbon, where he preached at the Royal Chapel. On several occasions in the 1640s the king asked him to undertake important diplomatic missions in various European capitals. He did so with success, but he decided to return to Maranhão in 1652 to continue his missionary work.

His sermons against the excesses of slave owners led to his expulsion from Brazil in 1661. Two sequences set up his forced departure. The first begins with a tableau representing São Luiz do Maranhão. Two low-angle shots reveal the tower of a church, and a sermon, preached on the fourth Sunday of Lent in 1657 and dealing with labor in pursuit of one's daily bread, begins in voiceover. Another shot shows African slaves waiting outside the church, unable to get in, followed by a statue of Christ, his arms bound in agony as the sermon ends.

The next sequence begins in what appears to be a well-lighted crypt, with a statue of the Virgin on the back wall. The film then cuts to a shot of Vieira preaching inside the church about injustice and the difficulty of governance. As he speaks, the camera slowly tracks in. The figure of a woman in a black cape with a skull in her left hand stands in an arched doorway to Vieira's right, and a statue of Christ on the cross hangs on the wall between them. The camera continues approaching Vieira until it focuses on him in a low-angle medium shot. Two men come and take him away. A shot of the crypt follows, with a white dove flying in the room. We next see him under arrest, kneeling and praying before an altar in a dark room. A young indigenous girl enters and offers him food. Then an intertitle, superimposed on a shot of the ocean, tells us that he has been expelled from Brazil. The silent figure in the doorway obviously represents death, while the dove flying free offers a visual contrast to Vieira's situation.

Back in Portugal, Vieira is called before the Inquisition, and the flashback that began with the film's initial dramatic sequence comes to an end. The rest of the film tells of Vieira's life from 1663 until his death in 1695: his involvement with the Inquisition (1663–67), his residence in Rome (1669–75), his return to Lisbon, the invitation to become the confessor of Sweden's Queen Cristina (played by Leonor Silveira), concerns about his health, his return to Brazil in 1681, his increasing loss of sight, and his death.

The film's concern with utopia involves utopian elements of religious thought and, perhaps more importantly, Vieira's ideas concerning prophecy and particularly the notion of the Fifth Empire, which Oliveira first broached in *Non ou a Vã Glória de Mandar.* The idea of the Fifth Empire involved the "consummation of the Empire of Christ on earth." It would last a thousand years until the coming of the antichrist, converting heretics, Muslims, pagans, and Jews and creating a world of peace and harmony. Vieira was summoned by the Inquisition in part because of his heretical ideas concerning Sebastianist millenarianism—which he transferred from King Sebastian to João IV, who died in 1656—his belief in the prophecies of Bandarra, and his supposed doctrinal errors.[31] Oliveira does not offer a detailed exposition of Vieira's ideas, although he does portray Vieira as unyielding in his beliefs and unrepentant in the face of the Inquisition.

Je Rentre à la Maison

With *Je Rentre à la Maison* (I'm going home; 2001), perhaps his lightest and most accessible film, Oliveira returns to the themes he explored in *Voyage to the Beginning of the World:* the relationship of art and life, aging, and mortality. Here he adds questions related to personal and professional ethics. The story is simple. After a theatrical performance, an actor, Gilbert Valence (Michel Piccoli), learns that his wife, daughter, and son-in-law have been killed in an automobile accident, and he is left to care for his grandson. He spends his time acting, drinking coffee in his favorite Parisian café, and occasionally playing with his grandson, even though their schedules don't coincide. He buys new shoes but loses them in a holdup. He turns down a lucrative role in a television series, but he accepts one as Buck Mulligan in a cinematic version of *Ulysses*, directed by an American (John Malkovich). Realizing that he is not up to the role, he walks off the set saying, "I'm going home."

Oliveira's love for the theater is evident in *I'm Going Home*. The film opens with a staging of an extended scene from Ionesco's *Exit the King* in which Valence plays the dying four-hundred-year-old King Berenger, who has difficulty coming to terms with his own impending death (Catherine Deneuve appears as Marguerite, Leonor Silveira as Marie, and Leonor Baldaque as Juliette). The blustery old monarch wonders why he was born, if his end is just to die, and he curses his parents for bringing him into the world. Inconsolable about the fleeting nature of life, he argues that he was born five minutes ago and married only three. Marguerite corrects him, trying unsuccessfully to get him to accept his situation. Although performed in a properly absurdist fashion, the segment raises issues about death, time, and immortality that are important for understanding the film as a whole.

Midway in the performance, three men enter the theater and make their way backstage, where they wait somberly for the play to end. They have come to tell Valence of the fatal accident. In many films, such a moment could be used melodramatically to play on spectator emotions. Discreet and understated as always, Oliveira prefers not to show the moment when Valence learns the truth. He is told offscreen as he is dressing, and we learn about it when one of the men tells the actors what has happened. Valence quickly leaves the theater without saying a word, and the narrative jumps ahead to "some time later" without dwelling on the tragedy. We next see Valence at home, looking out the window of his bedroom to his grandson Serge, who is riding a bicycle in the yard below. A single, static shot of Valence, in pajamas, sitting at his desk in the darkened room and looking at a picture of his deceased wife, before silently putting his head in his hands, eloquently and effectively paints a portrait of solitude, mourning, and the weight of responsibility.

Michel Picolli and Jean Koeltgen in *I'm Going Home* (Madragoa Filmes).

I'm Going Home is also an ode to Paris. It includes luminous shots of the Eiffel Tower, the Seine, various monuments and statues, and street scenes, including several shots of a carnival Ferris wheel and a merry-go-round, whose circularity is metaphorical. It is probably no accident that the first such image is an establishing shot of the Palais de Chaillot, which was long the headquarters of the Cinémathèque française. A scattered series of sequences offers a wonderful parody of ideological struggle that takes place in Valence's favorite café. He sits at a table near the door reading the left-wing newspaper *Libération,* which is not surprising for someone involved in the arts. As soon as he leaves, a conservatively dressed man sits down at the same table and unfolds the conservative *Le Figaro.* The same scene is repeated later in the film. The third time, however, Valence is still seated when the conservative gentleman walks in, and he is forced to sit at another table. When he sees Valence leave, he picks up his newspaper and his coffee and walks toward his traditional spot. Before he gets there, however, another man walks in and sits at the table, unfolding the middle-of-the-road *Le Monde.*

The first time Valence leaves the café, he walks down the street looking in shop windows. He stops before a shop where he looks at a print of the Scottish artist Jack Vettriano's *The Singing Butler.* The shopkeeper recognizes him, and she goes outside to talk. Since the camera is inside the store looking out, we see, but do not hear, their conversation. The shot continues when two girls ask for his autograph. The sound is not necessary, since we understand perfectly what is happening through the image alone, but the sequence reveals Oliveira's creative distance from mainstream cinematic conventions, in which the same thing is quite unlikely to happen. Valence again looks wistfully at the Vettriano print, in which a couple dances on a rainy beach while a butler and a maid hold umbrellas for them. Chopin's Waltz in A-flat major, Op. 69 No. 1, begins on the soundtrack—an appropriate accompaniment for the artistic image—and, perhaps recalling younger days, it seems as if he might want to dance. He walks on down the street and buys a new pair of shoes.

There follows a segment from act 4, scene 1 of *The Tempest,* in which Valence, as Prospero, says, "We are such stuff / As dreams are made on; and our little life / Is rounded with a sleep," reinforcing the film's concern with mortality. But the segment opens another theme, one that Oliveira briefly touched on in *Voyage to the Beginning of the World:* the possibility of a relationship between an older artist and a young actress. Sylvia (Leonor Baldaque) plays Miranda. After she exits the stage, she is clearly agitated. She looks on from the wings and smiles at Valence, but he returns her gaze with little enthusiasm, so she storms off and up the stairs to her dressing room. Her behavior is explained in the subsequent sequence.

Valence meets his agent, George (Antoine Chappey), at the café. Through most of their conversation, Oliveira's camera humorously focuses not on them but on their shoes under the table, as if it were a dialogue between shoes rather than men. George asks him how he is doing and whether he has considered finding someone, like a young actress, to help relieve his solitude. Valence finds the suggestion "roguish" and says that he is fine living with his grandson. Such a question brings up ethical issues for him that will reverberate in a later sequence in which George offers him a role in a television action series, alongside Sylvia, who has a crush on him and with whom his character will have an affair. Valence becomes indignant. He has never played such parts, regardless of how much they pay, and he refuses to start now. In this sense, Valence represents Oliveira's alter ego in his expression of a position that echoes the director's long-held opposition to commercial criteria in deciding which films to make.

After Valence takes leave of George at the café, he decides to walk home. As he walks down a dark street, a junkie with a knife holds him up. Valence has no money, so the thief takes his jacket, watch, and new shoes, of which he has been so proud. Later in the film, as Valence takes a cab home, he goes by the monument in the Place de la République on which the words "Liberté, Égalité, Fraternité" are written. The car roof cuts off his view in a subtle visual commentary about the state of things. Paris is not only the city of lights, it is also a city with dark corners, crime, and walls filled with graffiti; a city, like most metropolitan centers, that is not always the site of great liberty, equality, or fraternity.

In *I'm Going Home*, Oliveira again shows—through pacing, framing, and mise-en-scène—why he is a cinematic master. He is subtle, yet profound, and he constantly surprises. After Valence buys toy electric cars for his grandson and they play on the floor of the living room, there is a fifty-second nighttime shot of the outside of his house. All of the lights go off except one, then it goes off. A few seconds later, another light comes on, then it goes off again. There is no commentary, no voiceover, no sound except for an occasional car passing by. Through this simple image, Oliveira manages to give a sense of Valence's disquiet. The next morning, the phone rings, and Valence goes downstairs to answer. Rather than following him downstairs or cutting to the conversation, Oliveira prefers to leave his camera fixed on the bedroom door, with the conversation offscreen. To give but one more example, throughout much of the rehearsal of *Ulysses,* his camera focuses not on the actors going through their lines but rather on Malkovich sitting in the director's chair, his facial expressions subtly revealing his reaction to what he sees.

After Valence recognizes the futility of continuing in the role of Buck Mulligan and walks off the set, we again see him on the streets of Paris. Gone, however, are the elegant stores of his earlier walks. The sidewalk is cluttered with toys, and Valence looks absolutely disheveled, still in his costume and wig, muttering the lines he was unable to pronounce successfully. Passersby look at him as if he were mad. He goes into a bar (not his favored café) but walks out again without ordering anything.

When he arrives home, shoulders bent, seemingly carrying the weight of the world, Serge is riding his bike on the lawn. The boy looks at his grandfather with obvious concern and rushes over to the door as soon as Valence goes inside and starts to go up the stairs. The film's final shot is of Serge at the door, not of the aging actor who realizes that his career is over.

When asked about this ending, Oliveira responded that he focused on the boy because he had been secondary to that point, "but children have a sixth sense," and he perceives the disaster befalling his grandfather, "the representative of a past of wisdom and security who was falling apart before his startled eyes." He senses a great "responsibility for life coming down on him from the same staircase that his grandfather had climbed, disappearing at the top in defeat" (Parsi, "Entrevista"). It is hard to imagine a more eloquent and tender statement about age and mortality.

Porto da Minha Infância

Oliveira's sixty-two-minute *Porto da Minha Infância* (Porto of my childhood; 2001) is a hybrid film not unlike the earlier *O Dia do Desespero*. Although some critics have referred to it as a documentary, and although it includes documentary elements, the film is better described as a nostalgic evocation of certain aspects of the director's youth and young adulthood in the city of his birth. The view it offers of Porto is a personal one that is filtered through the director's memory and through brief contrasts with today's city, which is very different from the one where Oliveira grew up.

The film includes still photographs, archive footage of the city, footage from "Douro, Faina Fluvial" and *Aniki-Bóbó*, reconstructions of moments from Oliveira's past, recitations of poems, and the restaging of a scene of the popular play *Miss Dollar*, in which Oliveira himself plays the role of a burglar while one of his grandsons, playing Oliveira as a child, is in the family's loge in the audience. It includes a scene in which Agustina Bessa-Luís recites one of her own texts, as well as scenes involving some of the actors Oliveira has worked with: Leonor Silveira, Maria de Medeiros, Rogério Samora, Duarte de Almeida, and Joel Wallerstein.

Visually, *Porto da Minha Infância* includes a number of recurring images: waves crashing on the shore, the Douro River, and, most importantly, still images of the ruins of the house where Oliveira was born, which the director, who also serves as the film's narrator, describes as no more than a phantasm of the past. It also offers two recurring musical motifs: first, his wife Maria Isabel singing lines from the postromantic poet Guerra Junqueiro's poem of longing, "Regresso ao Lar" (Returning home), and segments from the composer Emmanuel Nunes's "Nachmusik I."[32] The film opens with a static shot of a conductor, his back to the camera, facing into darkness and illuminated from below, directing an invisible orchestra's performance of Nunes's piece.

In *Porto da Minha Infância*, Oliveira recalls his bohemian life as a young man, when he and his friends would go to different clubs in the city, ending at one that represented their "last recourse in finding an available *dama.*" He illustrates their lack of luck with a re-creation in which he (played by his grandson, Ricardo Trepa) and a friend are sitting in one of those clubs when two cocottes (Leonor Baldaque and Leonor Silveira) walk in and virtually ignore them. The Silveira character then walks over and sits down beside an older man, played by the president of the Cinemateca Portuguesa in Lisbon, João Bénard da Costa, who uses

Leonor Silveira in *Porto da Minha Infância*
(Madragoa Filmes).

the stage name Duarte de Almeida and who has appeared in numerous Oliveira films.

Oliveira devotes particular attention to his relationship with intellectuals such as Adolfo Casais Monteiro and Rodrigo de Freitas, who wrote the short story "Meninos Milionários" that formed the basis of *Aniki-Bóbó*. Casais Monteiro had been a central figure in the Presença movement of Portuguese modernism. In the 1930s he was arrested several times because of his opposition to the authoritarian Estado Novo, and he ended up leaving Portugal for Brazil, where he died in 1972. In homage to him, Oliveira recites passages from his 1946 book of verse, *Europa*. In addition, the film includes archival footage of men in the gardens outside of the Crystal Palace (which no longer exists) who, according to an intertitle, may be the poets Fernando Pessoa and Oliveira's close friend José Régio.

As one might expect, the cinema is central to *Porto da Minha Infância*. As Oliveira tells us, "From passion to passion the filmmaker was born." During the segment about his relationship with other intellectuals, the film shows the Majestic Café, where in 1934 Oliveira wrote the screenplay "Gigantes do Douro," a project he was unable to bring to fruition. When he speaks of one of the bridges over the Douro, it incorporates footage from "Douro, Faina Fluvial." He speaks about the garage where he and António Mendes improvised a laboratory in the process of making that same film, and he re-creates a brief scene of himself editing the film on a pool table. *Porto da Minha Infância* refers to Portugal's first filmmaker, Aurélio Paz dos Reis, and it includes footage of the country's first film, "Saída do Pessoal Operário da Camisaria Confiança" (Exit of workers from the Confiança Shirt Factory; 1896). The film juxtaposes past and present by having Paz dos Reis filming people walking out of the 2001 exhibition commemorating Porto's designation as the European Capital of Culture.

Near the end of the film, the camera travels down a modern thoroughfare alongside the Douro. As it reaches a curve, it pans to focus on a tile mural on a white wall, then closes in on its central figure: Prince Henry the Navigator. According to the critic Eduardo Cintra Torres, the significance of the mural is that Prince Henry was born in Porto, and with him was born an illustrious lineage, including the romantic writer Almeida Garrett (1799–1854) and Manoel de Oliveira, among many others. They each "conquered the world of their time" and constructed their own world. *Porto da Minha Infância* is a nostalgic look at the past through the eyes of memory, and yet Oliveira recognizes that those eyes are imperfect. Thanks to the cinema, we can see some of the places of his (and our) past, but with the passage of time, "many memories have been buried," just as his childhood home has become little more than a ruin.

O Princípio da Incerteza

In 2001, Agustina Bessa-Luís published the novel *O Princípio da Incerteza: Jóia de Família* (The uncertainty principle: Family jewel), which was planned as the first volume of a trilogy and for which she received the Grand Prize of the Portuguese Writers' Association. The novel served as the basis of Oliveira's *O Princípio da Incerteza* (2002).

When Oliveira learned of the award, which was announced while he was screening his film in Cannes, he explained that what had attracted him to the novel was the fact that "'the story is seen from the perverse side of contemporary society through one or two families and with frequently extraordinary and exceptional dialogue'" (qtd. in Henriques).

O Princípio da Incerteza returns to the novelistic universe of Bessa-Luís, to the geographical universe of the Douro, where Oliveira shot *Francisca* and *Abraham's Valley*, and to the moral landscape of those two films. In this purposely ambiguous tale, Oliveira pits good against evil in a story in which the boundaries between them are not always clear. The film deals with Camila (Leonor Baldaque), a young woman whose bourgeois family's fortune has been dilapidated by her father's gambling. His addiction had reached the point that he had attempted to use her sexual favors to pay off a gambling debt. Camila marries António Clara (Ivo Canelas), the heir to a substantial fortune, rather than her childhood crush, José Luciano (Ricardo Trepa), because of the social and financial benefits involved. "Portugal is a lottery," she says, and it is her time to win. Unbeknownst to any of them, António and José Luciano are brothers. Their mother, Celsa (Isabel Ruth), who had long served as a maid in the Clara household, secretly exchanged António with the stillborn son of the wealthy Rutinha (Cecília Guimarães) so that she would not suffer the pain of losing a son. António was thus raised "upstairs" as a son of the *haute bourgeoisie*, while José Luciano grew up "downstairs," the son of the family's maid. Celsa manages to arrange António's marriage with Camila, even knowing that José Luciano, the son who is recognized as her own, is in love with the young woman.[33] Marital bliss, however, is not to be achieved, in large part because of the presence of Vanessa (Leonor Silveira), who insinuates herself into the situation and becomes António's lover. Her expressed goal is to destroy Camila, or at least to make her suffer greatly, either because of envy or a thirst for power. Vanessa and José Luciano, in turn, are business partners, with a series of nightclubs and brothels. Things are never as clear as they might seem, however, which helps to explain the title and its relation to Bessa-Luís and Oliveira's use of Heisenberg's uncertainty principle: "The more precisely the position is determined, the less precisely the momentum is known in this instant, and vice versa."

Camila enters the marriage of convenience out of calculation, not love. And calculation guides her actions throughout, although she gives the appearance of being the traditional, conservative wife who helps her husband maintain the family's image. She acts passively in the face of repeated humiliations, primarily the constant presence of her husband's lover in her home. When, at a dinner party, Vanessa sits at the head of the table, Camila acts as if it were the most natural thing in the world. When she comes home one night and finds Vanessa in her living room with António, she does not react. She claims, in a conversation with her friend and adviser Daniel Roper (Luís Miguel Cintra), that António has beaten her. Vanessa calls her a "mutant" because she is unable to make her suffer. Nevertheless, her apparent acceptance of humiliation forms part of a broader strategy, which ultimately results in her victory. In this sense, Camila is quite unlike such previous Oliveira heroines as Benilde, Teresa, Francisca, and Ema.

O Princípio da Incerteza stages a struggle between the apparently passive Camila and the ostensibly devious and cynical Vanessa, a struggle in which social status and economic power are at stake. The critic António Cabrita has referred to their struggle as a fable in which Camila/Eve gradually internalizes the "shadows" of Vanessa/Lilith. At the beginning of the film Camila is, in the words of Celsa, "as pure as snow," and she is associated with a certain religiosity. The film opens on a rainy day with a long shot of a small chapel in the countryside. On the soundtrack, a violin plays a segment from Paganini's first "Caprice."

Camila slowly comes up from behind the chapel. As she reaches the front, she takes a key from under a stone and enters the chapel, closing the door behind her. A while later she comes back out, locks the door, replaces the key, and walks back down the hill out of sight. This action is repeated several times during the film, until it finally takes on an entirely different meaning from what we might surmise at the outset.

As is often the case in Oliveira's films, the story moves forward slowly, and primarily through extended conversations about society, love, relationships, and philosophical concepts. One of the key historical figures in the film is Joan of Arc, who becomes emblematic of Camila's struggle not only for power and wealth but also to define herself rather than be defined by António, Vanessa, or society. The point is made numerous times in the film that Camila is a prisoner or a slave to António. She initially reacts by playing the role. In a conversation with Vanessa, Camila tells her rival, "Your power is ephemeral; you have not yet reached the first stage of intelligence." When Vanessa asks what that might be, Camila responds, "It is goodness."

The association of Camila and Joan of Arc first occurs during a dinner party offered by António Clara prior to their engagement. Daniel Roper says that she reminds him of the French saint, warrior, and martyr. Later in the film, Camila goes to Porto to visit the cemetery where Roper is buried. There she talks about Joan of Arc, saying that there was a moment in her trial when she nearly became two people. She signed a retraction at the cemetery in St. Ouen and then began laughing. Four days later, she backtracked and was condemned to death. Rather then two women, Camila sees Joan of Arc as one, with a strong and powerful personality. When she returns to the small chapel near her home—this time the camera is on the inside waiting for her—we learn that inside is a cobwebbed statuette of Joan of Arc, to whom she prays for guidance. Camila then uses the power gained through her submission to punish those who had subjugated her. She becomes as much an angel as a demon, as much a martyr as an executioner (Silva).

One evening, Camila comes home to find the police in her house. They are questioning António, José Luciano, and Vanessa. José Luciano and Vanessa have apparently become involved in additional illegal activities. They have become indebted to a criminal element that is threatening to kill them if they do not pay. At one point, José Luciano tells

Camila to leave town, because she is too good to go through what is on the horizon. She insists repeatedly that "everyone thinks that I am good, but I'm not. I don't hurt anyone, it's a question of discipline, like covering your mouth when you yawn." Vanessa later asks Camila for money to help save her life, but Camila refuses, saying that she wouldn't give her money even under torture. She then lets out a laugh that Vanessa compares to that of Joan of Arc at St. Ouen.

Soon thereafter, António goes with José Luciano and Vanessa to one of their nightclubs. He is drunk. They ask him for money to help them out of their dilemma, but he too refuses, and he breaks off his relationship with Vanessa. José Luciano and Vanessa leave, and soon thereafter the innocuous jazzlike music is replaced by a techno beat. Four people enter in masks, dancing with bottles in their hands. They dance around António, pouring gasoline or some other combustible fluid on the floor. He is so drunk that all he can do his laugh. The men then set a match to it, and the nightclub becomes an inferno. António dies in the fire. During his wake, Camila takes a mask, much like the ones used by those who set the fire in the nightclub, and throws it into a wood-burning stove in the kitchen. At the end of the film, José Luciano is in jail, Vanessa has fled to Spain, and Camila is the heir to António's fortune. The final sequence shows her dressed in black in a lawyer's office. The lawyer tells her that he wants to learn everything about her case and, on a more personal level, everything about her. She smiles, as if she has accomplished everything she has set out to do. Her mask has come off.

As in other Oliveira films, language largely carries *O Princípio da Incerteza* forward. Not unusually, his camera is static throughout, except for a number of transitional shots in which it looks out the window of a moving train, which generally carries Camila to and from Porto. In such cases, the camera itself continues to be static; it is the vehicle that moves. Such transitions are frequently accompanied, on the musical soundtrack, by rather "demonic" passages from Paganini's "Twenty-four Caprices," particularly the sixth. Such musical passages are only used to reinforce transitional devices; there is no background music, as would be common in a Hollywood film. Although framing is not as hieratic as in films such as *Francisca*, and especially *Le Soulier de satin*, the mise-en-scène often tends toward the painterly, and the actors' mode of representation is anything but naturalistic, although they frequently show more emotion than in previous films. Oliveira continues his predilection for offering images of paintings and ornate interiors. At one point, for example, he cuts from Camila smiling at José Luciano from her window to the rather diabolical smile on the face of a baroque angel, thus subtly revealing her duplicity. The beautiful landscapes of the Douro region, particularly establishing shots and shots from the moving train, also play an important role, rooting the film in the land and the conventions of its society.

Um Filme Falado

Um Filme Falado (A talking picture; 2003) constitutes a reflection on the present and future of civilization, particularly within the context of the long-standing tension between Christianity and Islam. In this sense, it takes up some of the issues dealt with in *Non ou a Vã Glória de Mandar* in 1990. The narrative structure Oliveira uses for this strikingly profound and timely discussion is the following: Rosa Maria (Leonor Silveira), a university history professor, takes her daughter, Maria Joana (Filipa de Almeida), on a cruise to meet her husband and the girl's father in Bombay. Along the way, the mother explains the significance of the places they visit or pass by—Ceuta, Marseilles, Naples and Pompeii, Athens, Istanbul, Suez, and Aden—as well as such things as the meaning of myth, legend, and civilization. As they stop at ports along the way, three prosperous and well-known women of different nationalities board the ship: the entrepreneur Delphine (Catherine Deneuve) in Marseilles, the model Francesca (Stefania Sandrelli) in Naples, and the singer Helena (Irene Pappas) in Athens. The first half of the film is dedicated to Rosa Maria and Maria Joana's educational tourism; the second half to multilingual conversations at the dinner table of the ship's American captain, John Walesa (John Malkovich).

The date of the voyage, given in an explanatory title as the ship sets sail, contextualizes it implicitly in relation to 9/11: "In July 2001 a little girl accompanied by her mother, a distinguished history professor, crosses thousands of years of civilization while on their way to meet her father." *A Talking Picture* opens with a high-angle shot of people on a dock in Lisbon waving goodbye. Most immediately, they are waving goodbye to their friends and loved ones who are departing on a voyage to a yet-unknown destination. Metaphorically, they may be waving goodbye to Western civilization as we know it today. As Yaniv Eyny and

A. Zubatov have written, "[B]y the film's end, we begin to realise that Oliveira's reflections upon the past are actually reflections in a different sense: the film's many reference points in our early history and in the present-day voyage . . . stand as mirror-imaged bookends at the extreme ends of a long shelf sinking at a centre no longer able to withstand the pressure of its weighty volumes and illustrious titles." In Marseilles, the travelers' first port of call, Rosa Maria and her daughter walk toward a dock near the city center, and they see a small dog tied to a boat. The movement of the waves pulls the dog perilously close to the edge, and it struggles not to be pulled into the water. The dog's Sisyphean efforts to pull back from the brink constitute a wonderful visual metaphor for the state of Western civilization. It is not accidental that the dog is untied and "saved," so to speak, by a person associated with a knowledge of history, nor that the dog becomes associated with the little girl, upon whose shoulders the future rests. Nor is it coincidental that the ship captain, the one in charge of the voyage, is an American, a fact that is not particularly reassuring within the context of the film.

A *Talking Picture* offers multiple layers of historical, political, and cultural meaning through what might superficially seem to be a kind of cinematic travelogue. Not surprisingly, the most immediate historical reference involves Oliveira's native Portugal. As the ship leaves the Tagus River in Lisbon on its way to Bombay, Rosa Maria points out the Monument to the Discoveries on the banks of the river, with the figure of Prince Henry the Navigator, the "moving force" behind the voyages of discovery, at the forefront. In an allusion to the opening lines of Camões's *Lusiads*, she explains to her daughter that the navigators discovered new worlds "sailing hitherto unexplored waters." She then points out the Torre de Belém fortress, which was built between 1515 and 1520 to commemorate Vasco da Gama's voyage to India, which began in July 1497. Taking place during the same month, departing from the same city, and with the same destination—albeit via a different route—the voyage in A *Talking Picture* represents a modern echo of Vasco da Gama's journey, but in a different world with very different results.

The difference is prefigured in this initial sequence through another historical reference. It is a misty day, and Rosa Maria tells her daughter that the mist reminds her of the myth of King Sebastian, who would one day emerge from the mist to restore Portugal to its rightful place

Leonor Silveira and Filipa de Almeida in *A Talking Picture* (Madragoa Filmes).

in the world. She briefly explains that Sebastian disappeared in Alcácer-Kebir, a battle that was part of the king's crusade to convert the world to Christianity, starting with Muslims in northern Africa. Structuring the film from the outset, therefore, are the age-old conflict between Christianity and Islam and the question of imperial expansion or the spread of Western civilization.

As they sail by Ceuta, Rosa Maria explains that the Portuguese took the city from the Moors more than five hundred years earlier (in 1415, to be exact), although it is no longer Portuguese. In Marseilles, a plaque on the sidewalk commemorates the Greeks' arrival there in 600 BC, spreading civilization. In their visit to Pompeii, the film contrasts political or religious conflicts with natural cataclysms over which human beings have no control. In Athens the professor and her daughter visit the Acropolis, where they meet a Greek Orthodox priest. In Istanbul, the focus is on the Hagia Sophia cathedral, which was built in 537 by the Byzantine emperor Justinian and converted into a mosque in 1453. Inside, the camera lingers on Christian and Muslim iconography. As if to emphasize the film's concerns, hanging outside the cathedral, which is now a museum, is a banner announcing a photographic exhibit by Ahmed Ertu drawn from the book *Hagia Sophia: A Vision for Empires.*

In Suez, where they meet the actor Luís Miguel Cintra, playing himself, they discuss the European construction of the canal and the festivities that commemorated its inauguration.

Sailing through the Red Sea, Rosa Maria explains the biblical origins of the Arab people, descendents of Ishmael, son of Abraham and the slave girl Agar, and the later formation of nation-states through wars. When her daughter asks why men are so bad, Rosa Maria explains that the lust for power leads to war, which is precisely the point Oliveira broached in *Non ou a Vã Glória de Mandar*. In Aden, Rosa Maria explains that the Portuguese tried unsuccessfully to conquer the city to facilitate the sea route to Africa. In this sequence, the film again offers a visual contrast between Western and Islamic culture, primarily in terms of dress.

During the voyage, Delphine, Francesca, and Helena engage in multilingual conversation over dinner at the captain's table. These conversations, which begin at almost precisely the midway point of the film, constitute the second major component of *A Talking Picture*. The dinner guests speak, each in his or her own language (French, Italian, Greek, and English), about love, relationships, work, solitude, art, and theater. All four of them are childless, and Francesca and Helena in particular express regret at not having had children. Indeed, in the conversation the following evening in which Rosa Maria joins them, Francesca expresses deep sadness at the fact. As Eyny and Zubatov note, almost all of the characters Rosa Maria and her daughter encounter during the voyage are childless, starting with the fishmonger in Marseilles. In this sense, Maria Joana occupies a privileged space. "If the history lesson and the film are primarily hers, she is certainly burdened with an awesome responsibility as the single vessel capable of preserving the legacy of the past for the future" (Eyny and Zubatov). In this sense, Maria Joana represents more than a single little girl.

The dinner conversation soon turns toward such matters as language, civilization, and relations between the West and Arab countries. They find it strange, but somehow natural, that they are all speaking their own language and that they fully understand each other. The American captain says he knows fragments of languages, but he doesn't really need to use them, since almost everyone speaks English. It is no coincidence that the person in command is an American, whose language is later described as "implacable." Helena points out that although Greece is the birthplace of civilization, it is now largely forgotten. Delphine concurs and adds that the values of the French Revolution—liberty, equality, fraternity—have also been forgotten, particularly in light of the clash between the West and Arab countries, with its attendant fundamentalism.

The next evening, the captain invites Rosa Maria and Maria Joana to join them at his table. He gives Maria Joana a gift he purchased in Aden: a fully veiled Arab doll. After a brief conversation, again about language and, implicitly, power, the captain asks Helena to sing for the guests, and she agrees. She sings a nostalgic song about change that evokes a simpler age, which is reinforced by a panel of a grape harvest on the wall. The winds that blow, however, do not blow gently; they blow with a fury.

The final ten minutes of *A Talking Picture* transform it in such a way as to bring everything said about the clash of civilizations into high and horrific relief. While Helena is singing, an aide calls the captain and they leave the room. The captain returns a few minutes later and informs his dinner guests that in Aden terrorists managed to place two time bombs on board. A few minutes later comes the call to abandon ship, and the passengers leave the dining room to put on their life jackets. Rosa Maria and Maria Joana do the same, and they begin to follow the other passengers to the deck. Suddenly, Maria Joana breaks away from her mother and runs back to her cabin, where she has left the Arab doll. Rosa Maria frantically runs after her. When she reaches the cabin, she sees her daughter kneeling by the bed telling the doll, "Don't be afraid. I'll look after you." By the time they get to the deck, it is too late and all of the other passengers have embarked on lifeboats. From one of those boats the captain sees that they are still on the ship, and he yells for them to jump. Again, it is too late. The film ends with a freeze frame of the captain's face, looking in horror at what has happened, illuminated by the fire of the explosion.

Many things in *A Talking Picture* can be read allegorically: the crowd waving goodbye in Lisbon, the dog on the wharf in Marseilles, the child-lessness of most of the characters, the ship commanded by an American. One should not overlook the fact that the doll—perhaps an exotic trinket for some—is a gift from the captain. But the girl's role at the end, her attempt to save and protect her doll (obviously analogous to her own mother's role), also involves contact between cultures that, as the film shows, have long been in conflict. The doll is fully veiled; Joana Maria is wearing the Arab dress that her mother purchased in Aden. On one level, this contact represents a visualization of Helena's words during dinner concerning the need for a convergence of values between the West and the Arab world. Otherwise, it may be too late.

Oliveira links the events of the film and recent acts of terrorism not only to the history of Western civilization but also, and more specifically, to the history of Portugal. On the dining room wall behind the captain is a painting of what appears to be Lisbon as it might have looked at the time of Vasco da Gama's voyage to India. When Maria Joana runs back to get her doll, she and her mother pass a large painting of Vasco da Gama three times. Each time, the camera lingers on the painting. In *Non ou a Vã Glória de Mandar,* Lieutenant Cabrita refers to the voyages of discovery as representing one of Portugal's great gifts to the world. In his view, they were humanism in practice, if not theory. The painting on the wall is one of optimism and promise, with da Gama looking out toward the future, and the sun's rays forming a cross as it shines over an island in the ocean. *A Talking Picture* shows how distant that hope is from the reality of the contemporary world.

O Quinto Império: Ontem como Hoje

With *O Quinto Império: Ontem como Hoje* (The Fifth Empire: Yesterday as today; 2004), Oliveira revisits the work of José Régio and questions of history and utopia that he had explored in diverse ways in *Le Soulier de satin, Non ou a Vã Glória de Mandar, Palavra e Utopia,* and *A Talking Picture.* The film is based on Régio's three-act play *El-Rey Sebastião* (1949). The change in title, however, points toward a reading in light of present circumstances in which dreams of empire and utopia, at times based on a supposed predestination, involve age-old conflicts between cultures and religions. When the film was screened in Venice, some associated Sebastian with George W. Bush, and Oliveira himself has said that Bush has a "Sebastianist" inclination in his expressed desire to spread democracy and freedom around the globe in his own version of the Fifth Empire (Câmara; Dacosta; Neto).

Whereas in previous films Oliveira included sometimes extensive references to King Sebastian I (1544–78) in the course of narratives

Luís Miguel Cintra and Ricardo Trepa in *O Quinto
Império* (Madragoa Filmes).

dealing with different historical and dramatic situations, the ill-fated
Portuguese king is the central focus of *O Quinto Império*. The story takes
place almost entirely in an antechamber in his castle, perhaps during a
single day and night, and it involves conversations the king has with his
advisers; his grandmother, Queen Catarina (Catherine of Hapsburg);
two court jesters; and perhaps most importantly Simão Gomes, the
"Sapateiro Santo" (Holy Cobbler), a friend of the cobbler Gonçalo Anes,
or Bandarra (1550–56), whose prophecies inspired the utopian vision of
António Vieira. In Shakespearean fashion, there are also disembodied
voices that some suspect are the spirits of Portugal's first king, Alfonso
Henriques, and his son Sancho I, while Simão tells Sebastian that the
voices may well come from inside the king himself.

Starting from the first shot of *O Quinto Império*, Oliveira creates,
partially through an exquisite play of light and darkness, a phantasmagoric atmosphere in which the frontier between reality and dreams is
not always clear. While one must assume that Sebastian's counselors, his
grandmother, and the two jesters form part of his physical reality as king,
Simão Gomes may emerge from the king's imagination, his dreams, or

his unconscious. The disembodied voices, although heard by a number of people, and not only the king, obviously help establish the spectral atmosphere from the outset.

In its portrait of the young king (played by Ricardo Trepa) at a moment when he is clearly considering the disastrous imperialist crusade that culminated in the battle of Alcácer-Kebir, *O Quinto Império* focuses on motivation. Why would Sebastian undertake such a campaign against the advice of his grandmother the queen, his council of state, and the mysterious, disembodied voices? The counselors offer multiple reasons why he should not pursue the crusade: the kingdom is poor, his people are tired and poorly clothed, the forces at his disposal are insufficient, his allies cannot provide additional men, he doesn't have the funds to hire mercenaries, there would be a huge risk in doing so even if he had the money, the nobility cannot afford to pay for the adventure, and even if he wins, which they see as unlikely, it would be impossible for him to sustain the occupation. Is it legitimate, one of his counselors asks, for him to lose the kingdom because of a personal fantasy?

The answer the play and the film offer to the question of motivation lies not in rational political action but rather in the king's obsessive personality, which includes more than a small dose of megalomania, and particularly in history and myth, that is, in Sebastian's obsession with his place in Portuguese history and with the myths that have surrounded him, both in terms of his genesis and his legacy. The grandson of King João III (1521–57), Sebastian became heir to the throne when his father, Prince João of Portugal, the only surviving son of João III, died two weeks before his birth in 1554. Since Sebastian's birth was necessary for the continuity of the Avis Dynasty, he was known as the Desejado, or Desired One. When João III died in 1557, Sebastian was proclaimed king under a regency headed initially by his grandmother, Queen Catarina. He assumed power at the age of fourteen, and he disappeared in northern Africa ten years later. After he died, he also became known as the Encoberto, or Hidden One, who would one day return to restore Portugal's grandeur.

Sebastian's obsession with his place in history becomes evident almost from the outset when he visits the tombs of previous Portuguese monarchs as well as in his almost fetishistic fixation with the sword of the founder of the Portuguese nation, Afonso Henriques, who, in 1139, defeated five Moorish kings in the Battle of Ourique. Sebastian wants to join the heroic kings of the past and, if possible, exceed their accomplishments and conquests. This is no doubt the meaning of the film's final, oneiric scenes, when statues of past monarchs come to life and surround the young king. And yet his desire for the glory of command is vain, as Oliveira showed in *Non ou a Vã Glória de Mandar.*

Sebastian's sense of predestination becomes evident near the beginning of the film when he asks one of his noblemen to read verses of a poet who had sung "the kingdom's glories," a poet apparently "of great worth." He is referring to Luís de Camões, who had published the first edition of *The Lusiads* in 1572, six years before the disaster in Alcácer-Kebir, when Sebastian, to whom it is dedicated, was eighteen years old. The nobleman reads the following stanza from the epic poem's dedication:

And you, my boy King, guarantor
Of Portugal's ancient freedoms,
And equal surety for the expansion
Of Christendom's small empire;
You, who have the Moors trembling,
The marvel prophesied for our times,
Given to the world, in God's eternal reign,
To win for God much of the world again. (6)

After the nobleman finishes reading, Sebastian stands and repeats the final line—"To win for God much of the world again"—clearly taken up with his own myth.

In Régio's play and Oliveira's film, the Sapateiro Santo, Simão Gomes (Luís Miguel Cintra), is the only person Sebastian listens to, although he sometimes speaks in a prophetic voice that the king does not understand. Simão agrees with those who counsel against reckless adventurism against Islam, but he shows the king the only path he can take to reconcile his historical role and the myths that surround him: follow his destiny and allow himself to be annihilated, or, in other words, commit suicide. Only thus can he forever remain the Desejado and the Encoberto. Only through death can he achieve the immortality he desires. If, in *Non ou a Vã Glória de Mandar* and *A Talking Picture,* Oliveira reveals, in a broad sense, the terrible legacy of messianic inclinations

Manoel de Oliveira filming *O Quinto Império*
(Madragoa Filmes).

and utopian desires such as that of Sebastian, in *O Quinto Império* he
returns to its genesis in megalomania, obsession, and irrationality.

As might be expected, given its source text, in *O Quinto Império*
Oliveira returns to a highly theatrical mode of representation, with exquisite mise-en-scène and normally frontal framing. The film begins with
the camera slowly ascending one of the castle's exterior walls while Carlos
Paredes's Portuguese guitar is heard on the soundtrack. One of the film's
most beautiful shots, with the camera following, in slow motion, the arc
of a sword that Sebastian has thrown into the air—is also accompanied
by the same musician. The use of Paredes's music represents an homage
to the great composer and musician, who passed away in July 2004, as
Oliveira was completing the film.

Epilogue

Since the Venice Film Festival honored Oliveira for his lifetime achieve-
ments, the Portuguese director has had two additional films debut in the
same venue. *Espelho Mágico* (Magic mirror, 2005) is based on Agustina
Bessa-Luís's novel *A Alma dos Ricos* (The soul of the wealthy, 2002),

the second volume of the trilogy *O Princípio da Incerteza*. Starring Leonor Silveira, Leonor Baldaque, Ricardo Trepa, Isabel Ruth, and Marisa Paredes, and produced by José Miguel Cadilhe rather than Paulo Branco, with whom Oliveira had worked since *Francisca,* the film tells the story of Alfreda (Silveira), a wealthy woman whose desire is to see an apparition of the Virgin Mary. José Luciano (Trepa) provides continuity with *O Princípio da Incerteza,* since he goes to work for Alfreda shortly after his release from prison. The film's American release took place in the 2005 Chicago International Film Festival. *Belle Toujours* (2006) renders homage to Luís Buñuel, Jean-Claude Carrière, and their *Belle de jour* (1967) by taking up two of the characters—Husson (Michel Piccoli) and Séverine (now played by Bulle Ogier rather than Catherine Deneuve)—forty years later. Near the century mark, Manoel de Oliveira has a number of projects on his agenda, including an adaptation of Oscar Wilde's *The Picture of Dorian Gray* and another based on a short story by Eça de Queiroz (in Lisbon's *Diário de Notícias,* 28 January and 22 April 2005). Then he might take a brief vacation before beginning yet another.

Notes

1. The Jesuits were expelled from Portugal in 1910, shortly after the declaration of the Republic. In *Viagem ao Princípio do Mundo* (Voyage to the beginning of the world; 1997), Oliveira's alter ego, the director Manoel, played by Marcelo Mastroianni, talks about his experience in the boarding school in La Guardia.

2. Oliveira appears briefly in *Acto da Primavera, Amor de Perdição, A Divina Comédia, Voyage to the Beginning of the World, Inquietude, Porto da Minha Infância,* and João Botelho's *Conversa Acabada* (1981), plus a number of short films. For a complete list, see Matos-Cruz 165–84.

3. Unless otherwise indicated, all translations are my own.

4. One of the treatments from this early period, for a project titled "Bruma" (1931), can be found in *Alguns projectos não realizados e outros textos de Manoel de Oliveira* (11–15).

5. Critics have made much of a scene in *A Canção de Lisboa* in which a woman in a dress shop tries on a dress that has the following sign attached to its derriere: "Ocasião—95:00—Estado Novo" (Sale—95 escudos—New State). One might also mention the scene in which the protagonist Vasco Leitão, played by the comic actor Vasco Santana, rails against the *fado,* repeating several times that

he is "antifadista," which is phonetically close to "antifascista," or "antifascist."
See Granja 210–11.

6. The screenplay has been published in *Alguns projectos não realizados e
outros textos de Manoel de Oliveira*.

7. The Fundo de Cinema and the censorship office both functioned within
the dictatorship's Secretariat of Information, Popular Culture, and Tourism,
which explains the close connection between financing and censorship.

8. The Calouste Gulbenkian Foundation was created in the mid-1950s by the
will of the Armenian-born Calouste Gulbenkian, who had resided in Lisbon since
1942. Since its inception it has been dedicated to promoting art and culture in
Portugal. See "Manoel de Oliveira."

9. On Portuguese Cinema Novo, see *O Cinema Novo Português 1960/1974*.

10. Duarte the Almeida is the stage name of the critic João Bénard da Costa,
a well-known intellectual and a longtime friend of Manoel de Oliveira. At the
time of this writing, he is serving as director of the Cinemateca Portuguesa in
Lisbon.

11. The sequences from "A Velha Casa" and the screenplay of "O Caminho"
can be found in *Alguns projectos não realizados e outros textos de Manoel de
Oliveira*.

12. The novel has been translated into English with the title *Doomed Love*.

13. Obviously, the image may not necessarily capture certain metaphorical
aspects of a writer's description, although it may create metaphors of its own.

14. In reality, Manoel de Oliveira serves as a third narrator, not only in the
sense of director qua narrator but also in a more literal or textual sense. It is
his voice that utters the final words, taken from Castelo Branco's *Memórias
do Cárcere*. The television version also used Teresa's sister, Rita, to provide
transitions between the six episodes, summarizing what had occurred in the
previous one.

15. Other films shot entirely or partially in French include *Mon Cas* (1986),
The Convent (1995), *Party* (1996), *Voyage to the Beginning of the World* (1997),
La Lettre (1999), *I'm Going Home* (2001), *A Talking Picture* (2003), and *Belle
Toujours* (2006). In this sense, *Le Soulier de satin* helped establish Oliveira's
reputation as a European, rather than only a Portuguese, director. The film was
made possible in part by a two-million-franc advance from the French Minister
of Culture Jack Lang (Baecque and Parsi 82).

16. Claudel's stage directions and the Announcer's introduction read as follows: "First Day. Short trumpet-call. 'The Scene of this play is the world, and
more especially Spain at the close of the Sixteenth, unless it be the opening of
the Seventeenth, Century . . .' Another short trumpet-call. A prolonged whistle
or hoot, as though a ship were putting about. Curtain rises" (xxvi).

17. The photographic illustrations from *Le Soulier de satin, Mon Cas, Non
ou a Vã Glória de Mandar,* and *Abraham's Valley* included herein offer three
variations on their gaze.

18. I am not suggesting that Oliveira was in any way influenced by Andrade or his film. Indeed, the two directors' aesthetic, ideological, and political stances are very different.

19. An excerpt from Oliveira's homage is included in the DVD package *L'integrale Jean Vigo*, released by Gaumont in 2001.

20. In *The Lusiads*, Venus also descends supported by swans, but she is seated on a chariot or *carro*, not on a shell (canto 9; 36).

21. Oliveira says much the same thing in the interview that appears in the DVD version of the film, released by Atalanta Filmes in 2001.

22. Her words are from canto 9, stanzas 37 and 38 of *The Lusiads*.

23. Two versions of *Abraham's Valley* exist. One, 187 minutes long, was exhibited in the Cannes Film Festival and released commercially. The other, 210 minutes long, restores four sequences that Oliveira had eliminated in an attempt to make the film meet festival regulations. The shorter version, unfortunately dubbed into French, is available on DVD, released in the United States by Vanguard. The longer version, which I have used, has been released on DVD by Madragoa Filmes in Lisbon.

24. In 1996 Oliveira also made a twenty-five-minute documentary about his native Porto, "En une Poignée de Mains Amies" (In the hold of friendly hands) with the French filmmaker Jean Rouch.

25. From the "Director's Statement" on the film's official website, www .madragoafilmes.pt/oconvento/#.

26. Manuel Cintra Ferreira writes that at such moments Mastroianni, in the foreground, seems like an "amplification" of Oliveira, who remains discreetly in the background. Stéphane Bouquet suggests that Oliveira moves about like a *ludion*, a wandering figure, actor, or entertainer.

27. The film was Paulo Rocha's *O Desejado-As Monhanhas da Lua* (*Les Montagnes de la Lune;* 1987).

28. Oliveira's *Party* also opens with Pappas singing in Greek on the soundtrack, and *A Talking Picture* is multilingual, with dialogue in Portuguese, English, Greek, Italian, and French. The Pappas character also sings a traditional Greek song in the film.

29. From the interview with Oliveira on the DVD of *A Carta*, released by Madragoa Filmes in 2003.

30. Three years after *La Lettre*, Oliveira again collaborated with Pedro Abrunhosa by directing a music video for the composer/singer's "Momento, uma espécie de céu" (Moment, a kind of heaven), a plaintive song about time, solitude, and, as the composer puts it, the permanence of the moment, with "death being the supreme moment" (*Os momentos do MOMENTO*). Oliveira's video can be viewed at Abrunhosa's site: www.abrunhosa.oninet.pt/.

31. The bibliography on Vieira is extensive. For an extensive discussion, see Cohen. For a brief overview, see the online Catholic encyclopedia at New Advent: www.newadvent.org/cathen/15415d.htm.

32. Oliveira himself sings brief passages from "'The Toreador Song," from Bizet's *Carmen,* and "Fado das Mãos," by Arnaldo Leite and Carvalho Barbosa, although they do not constitute recurring motifs.

33. If one wanted to complicate things even more, one might consider the fact that Leonor Baldaque is Augustina Bessa-Luís's granddaughter, whereas Ricardo Trepa, who plays José Luciano, is Manoel de Oliveira's grandson.

"A Mental Conception of Cinema"

An Interview by Jean A. Gili

JEAN A. GILI: Let's begin by talking about your latest film, *A Divina Comédia* [1991]. Among its sources are the Bible, Dostoevsky, Nietzsche, and the Portuguese writer José Régio, from whom you borrowed the figure of the prophet. In which work does the prophet appear?

MANUEL OLIVEIRA: He's from a play written in the early 1950s called *A Salvação do Mundo* [The world's salvation], a poetic work dealing with a kingdom inhabited by very strange people. The story includes a prophet who resists the superficial life we lead. He is the mirror of our mundane world. He says wise things, and he carries a book that he calls the fifth gospel. At a certain moment, in a tavern frequented by the king disguised as an ordinary subject, he unintentionally leaves his book on a table. When he returns, someone has indiscreetly opened it and has seen that it is blank. The prophet then offers his explanation: words and matter corrupt the spirit. Unfortunately, one cannot have spirit without matter. There is no pure spirit.

JAG: How did you come to the idea of bringing together texts from different cultures?

MO: They are not from different cultures; their source is the same. Their relationship has to do with the problem of resurrection, whether in Dostoevsky's *Crime and Punishment* or *The Brothers Karamazov* or in Nietzsche's *Anti-Christ*. Everything derives from the question of Original Sin according to our Western vision or education. The problem is the same for those who believe and for those who don't. It's not a matter of belief, which is another question. Another life either exists, or it doesn't. The problem of resurrection goes totally beyond our weak understanding. Some think that everything ends with death, that there is nothing after death except darkness. Others think the opposite. They are opposing positions. That in itself poses the question of values. Are values absolute or not? If there is something beyond life, some kind of justice, it is necessary to respond to such questions. If there is nothing, one can do whatever one wants; that's what Ivan Karamazov says. I didn't add anything. Dostoevsky is wonderful. The two texts that I chose go together perfectly with regard to resurrection, belief, power, the will to control, to command, even to the point of wanting to be superior to one's own God. All of that surprised me very much. They are admirable texts that are considered the best of their respective authors; they are anthological texts of universal literature.

JAG: Did you shoot the film in continuity?

MO: No, I shot the last scene first in order to take advantage of the light. It was the end of autumn; winter would soon come, and the leaves would fall. As a guarantee, we had to shoot that scene quickly. Then, I waited a few days to continue shooting. Things are never very well organized. I have the same problem with my next film. There are winter scenes, and I am still writing the script. I need to shoot some scenes that take place in winter before I finish the script.

JAG: What film is that?

MO: It's called *Abraham's Valley*. It is distantly based on *Madame Bovary*. I'm still writing the screenplay. It departs significantly from Flaubert's novel, even if it partakes of the same spirit. The story takes place in the present in the Douro region.

JAG: For *A Divina Comédia*, I imagine that it was difficult to get all of the actors together.

MO: In fact, there were a lot of problems with availability. They are stage actors. Maria de Medeiros works in Paris, and she was available only on certain days. Maria José Pires, who plays the role of Martha, is a great international concert pianist. She had contracts that forced her to abandon the shooting. It was always difficult to get them all together. Sometimes I would take advantage of their presence to shoot them all together when, in the counter-shot, I had only one actor because the others had left. That often posed problems for the film's construction, but as a whole everything worked out. One actor fell ill during the shooting: Ruy Furtado, who plays the role of the director of the psychiatric hospital. He was a great actor and friend, but unfortunately he passed away.

JAG: You were forced to replace him for the scene with the Karamazov brothers. You yourself appear in the sequence, which is rather strange in the sense that it is one of the film's key sequences.

MO: Yes, that's true. It's precisely the moment when I did not want to replace him, much less take his place. I did not want to embody that character, but at the same time I had to do so. I didn't choose another actor because of my respect for Ruy Furtado. I didn't want to put anyone else's name in the credits for the role of the director of the psychiatric hospital. So I thought it would be best if I did it myself. Like him, I don't have hair, and with the glasses I thought it might work. When he became ill we waited a while hoping he would recover, but his doctor took away all hope, and I was forced to take on the role. Ruy Furtado died a few days later, and we all went to his funeral. He was a very important figure in Portuguese cinema.

JAG: In the sequence in which you appear as an actor, Ivan Karamazov tells the director that he is "skeptical, rebellious, and desperate." Isn't that your own question about skepticism, revolt, and despair?

MO: No, that's not what I meant to say. I would not want to be that character who, I believe, has no faith. The Jesuit António Vieira—one of the writers who inspired me in *Non ou a Vã Glória de Mandar*—says that hope is the last recourse of nature. When one loses hope, one loses everything. One becomes a skeptic and sees only despair and death. One cannot live without hope, even if it is not necessarily hope in God. It is important to have hope in something, an ideology, a belief, even an incorrect ideology. We are all moved by a hope that makes us live, we all live confident that the sun will rise tomorrow. We cannot be certain of that, but hope makes us see the sun rising on a new day. If not, everything is over.

JAG: Do you feel outraged?

MO: I am filled with doubt, and one might say that I am a little outraged, even if I don't like that word. Generally speaking, I am truly disquieted with regard to mankind. Human beings are free vis-à-vis their acts, not really for their destiny, but for what they do. Their behavior is the result of their will. There are terrible attitudes in the political realm as well as in the civil realm—behavior toward children, for example—that revolt me, since I belong to the human family . . .

JAG: Shooting a film based on a patchwork of literary references may seem paradoxical given that the cinema is above all a succession of images.

MO: A film is not just images. It is a mistake to think that. Why just images? Images are for the eyes, but not for the ears. We have both senses, we can see and we can hear. When one gives a speech or reads a text, one might say that they already exist and that there is nothing artistic about it. But when one films a face, one can also say that it already exists and that there is nothing artistic about filming it; it is a photograph. If one chooses a landscape, it is already there; if one chooses a décor, it is also already there. But the manner of filming, the choice of lighting, the choice of the voice that will say a text, the manner of saying it, its context, all of this is very important, and it ensures that it is not just a simple reproduction. The soundtrack is becoming increasingly important in the cinema. Color, sound, and words are cinema's wealth, they constitute a direct transmission of thought, abstractly but also visually. Why give preponderant importance to the image or the sound? The director may prefer one over the other at any given moment. I believe that it is legitimate to privilege one of the two components, to give the same cinematic value to one or the other. The cinema started with movement, "kino," but the real difference between photography and the cinema is not movement, it is the context of each shot. Each shot resembles a photograph, but it is within a context, while the photograph is out of context. The context is within the photograph, while in the cinema the context is outside of the shot, it is in the relationship between shots. That is the great difference between cinema and photography. It is not movement, or rather it is movement as a link between shots and above all as the possibility of introducing sound. If there is no movement, there can be no music; sounds do not exist without movement. The image, yes; it can be stopped, as in a tableau. One does not need movement to show an image, but one does for sound. One might say, therefore, that sound is more cinematic than the image.

JAG: In some of your texts you have noted your admiration for silent cinema of the 1920s.

MO: Yes, but in terms of language. If one adds sound, which did not exist in the 1920s, one sees that sound followed cinematic language. One cannot apply the type of language that characterized the 1920s to sound. That's what is interesting. The earth is round, and everything goes around, not in a circular fashion but rather in an helical manner, in a spiral. That is, when one repeats something, that moment is already another moment, another time, it is the same but it's different. There is nothing new, and we always return to the same point. But in artistic expression, what is new is the way one organizes things, it is the way of seeing the same things in a different manner. Love is always love, crime is always crime, a woman is always a woman, a man is always a man; behaviors do not change. There are constant behaviors and others that change according to mores, epochs, fashions. . . . But we have moved away from *A Divina Comédia*.

JAG: Before *A Divina Comédia, Non ou a Vã Glória de Mandar* was an equally original undertaking.

MO: *Non ou a Vã Glória de Mandar* is a reflection on Portugal's history. The history of each country is not just the specific history of a certain country, it is also part of world history. To put it another way, it is a fragment of the history of humanity. One can say therefore that nothing happens without a reason, that everything has a meaning. How? Everything occurs in relation to the end, an enigmatic but absolutely essential end, an end that is very important for man himself. What is it? What is going to happen? Win a battle. Lose a battle. Be a hero. To be a hero, one needs to kill a lot of enemy soldiers. That's what concerns me, that makes me reflect. The one who doesn't kill anyone is killed. Did he die innocent? What is the verdict? Is life only a terrestrial adventure? If everything is over with death, everything is permitted. If there is something beyond life, if there is a justice that transcends us, then we are responsible, and everything that takes place here becomes less important in relation to eternal judgment. To lose a war, to be unhappy, to be very rich, to be a hero, to hold great power, what is the meaning of all of this? Who are we? What will happen after death? At the end of the film, I don't provide an answer. I appeal to my education—an education that belongs to Western civilization—and I question it. I confront opposing elements of everything that is the history of humanity according to our Judeo-Christian, Greco-Roman historical conception, a civilization that continues today under the command of America. The question of power is not important; something else is important. That's the divine comedy. When one doesn't understand, one calls that which is tragic divine.

JAG: *Non ou a Vã Glória de Mandar* in fact poses numerous questions about human destiny.

MO: I'm thinking about publishing something about the film. The idea came to me during a debate with the participation of João Bénard da Costa, Jacques Parsi, a professor of history, a film critic, and the public. I wrote an essay about the film. I really like the idea of the book because the text allows for a greater understanding of the film. A painter and three writers were concerned about the history of Portugal and reflected on the meaning of history. In 1450, Nuno Gonçalves's polyptych represents episodes in the life of Saint Vincent. I established a relationship between Saint Vincent and the history of Portugal. Nuno Gonçalves is thus the first. Then there is Luís de Camões with *The Lusiads*, Father António Vieira with *The Fifth Empire,* and finally Fernando Pessoa. The story on which *Non ou a Vã Glória de Mandar* is based is, shall we say, the coincidence of the prophecies that occur in the polyptych of Saint Vincent and the books of Pessoa, prophecies that were fulfilled. They said certain things that were fulfilled after their death. I propose that interpretation thanks to a new interpretation of Nuno Gonçalves's painting. I will publish the book one way or another because it is very important for me, it is a good contribution to the understanding of the history of Portugal, the film itself, and all of its strange and mysterious coincidences. I even use a hidden personage such as the philosopher Sampaio Bruno and an interpretation of *saudade* [nostalgia] according to the writer Teixeira de Pascoaes. Everything is connected. It is strange, but I find the sentiment of *saudade* in some films I have seen recently, such as Godard's *Germany Year 90 Nine Zero*, and Angelopoulos's *The Suspended Step of the Stork*. *Saudade* is a Portuguese sentiment that travels. There is something hidden that will return. It is this coincidence that makes me think of some things that escape us.

JAG: Your life as a filmmaker has been quite unique, with few films until the age of sixty, and ten features after 1971. You have a sort of compulsion or unflinching will to recuperate what you were unable to do when you were young. We are talking about *A Divina Comédia*, and you have already finished another film and are preparing yet another. . . .

MO: I have loved the cinema since I was a child; I always loved moving images. When sound arrived, I was obviously against it, since at the time people were trying to define cinematic specificity: "Say everything through the image." Since the advent of sound cinema and the possibility of using speech and sounds, things are easier, more beautiful, and more expressive. That may seem dumb, but I like that possibility a great deal. The way to deal with these problems changes with age. I grew up with the cinema, and it grew up with me; we walked together. The evolution of film criticism has been considerable, and my mental evolution has also been great. When I began shooting "Douro, Faina Fluvial," at the end of the 1920s, I had a very precise idea about what the cinema should be, perhaps too precise. Today, I am a different person, I have different ideas, which are also precise, but with a lot of doubts. I'm not sure how to express myself, but let's say that there is something that gives me a certain stability, a certain security in my work. I know that I should do things in a certain way. I may achieve results that are better or worse, or not achieve that which I want to achieve, but that's what I need to do. There is a very great force inside me. I don't advance blindly, I know very well that I should do things in this manner. It is not a rule or a theory, it's my viewpoint or impulse, but it's good for me. During the years when I didn't film, I wrote screenplays and thought a lot about the cinema. That gave me a very mental conception of the cinema. Previously I had a more technical view. Today, I have a truly mental vision, just as Leonardo da Vinci's painting was mental. The mind rules. Of course, there are feelings, but I always seek to eliminate them as much as possible, although I can't do so entirely. I try to eliminate the subjective, the sentimental, the psychological. I want to face the facts, as Dostoevsky said through Ivan.

I stick to facts. If I try to understand them, I change them. That's what I want; I am here, but what I want is not to be here. They are things that are there, not me. My choice is pretty much that.

JAG: In short, during the years when you didn't film, you stored up creativity.

MO: Yes, perhaps. I was engaged in a long process of reflection. I gradually became aware of what I wanted to do. There are films in which I did not have a clear sense of what I was doing, such as *Acto da Primavera*. I understood what I had done after the fact. It's a film that I shot somewhat through intuition, but it's a very important film in my work. After it, I became aware of the nature of cinema, the value of language. Everything comes from that film, but at the moment of shooting I worked intuitively.

JAG: How did the idea of filming a popular representation of the Passion of Christ come about?

MO: I was shooting "O Pão," a documentary about the making of bread, and I was looking for some windmills when I saw erected crosses. It was around Easter, the weather was bad, and the peasants had left the crosses in place because they had not been able to put on the spectacle because of rain. They planned to do it a few days later. I asked what was happening, and they explained that the representation would take place the following Sunday. Since I was still in the area, I went to see it, and I was so surprised that I immediately thought about filming it. The peasants agreed to put on a special performance for me. I used the same actors, and I called others to interpret secondary figures, people who had not participated in it before. The film is not a documentary; I redid everything. The peasants expressed confusing things. I took the text and asked them to clarify what they wanted to represent. Starting from our discussions, I put a bit of order in the representation. I would ask "Is that it?" and they would respond, "Yes, that's good." Therefore, the modifications took place with their agreement. This representation of the Passion of Christ was a special experience that opened new paths for me.

JAG: In *Acto da Primavera*, we see the sound truck and you at the camera; in *Benilde*, we see the back of the studio set before going inside it; in *A Divina Comédia*, the final image is of the clapboard. You show the cinema being made. Do you feel the need to tell the spectator: "This is a film"?

MO: Yes, it's a film, it's not reality. But what's a film? A film is a phantasm, it is not life. On the other hand, life doesn't exist; it too is a phantasm. Without books, without historians, without memory, not a trace would be left. The moment is emphemeral. To struggle against oblivion, humans have a need to remake what touches them, a will to preserve that which is important to them. It begins by telling a friend what has happened. Then the friend will tell another. One can represent what has happened, that's theater; one can represent the different dramas one sees on the street. But these theatrical representations are equally fleeting, as is life. The cinema possesses a very important element: the ability to capture things. Television can transmit directly, but then the event is lost. When television is recording, it comes close to the cinema. The cinema fixes that which is filmed. In this sense it recalls primitive painting, rupestrian paintings in caverns, with their desire to create images of reality. It's the same thing as the pleasure of showing a family album, photographs of children, relatives, of one's spouse. We feel a sort of necessity in relation to the events and people of whom we want to preserve a trace. We want to stop the moments that touch us; the others disappear. I once asked myself: "Do the moments of my life that I forget really belong to me? Are they really important or not? Do they continue to exist in my subconscious, and do they determine what we retain in our memory?" All of this is a bit of a mystery. In relation to this kind of reflection, I reject traditional cinema, the American-style film that wants to give us the impression that life is on the screen, not outside of it. *We make you feel the characters' emotions, we make you feel sympathy for the bandit or the policeman.* The director can do as he wishes, not as the spectators might want him to do. For him, life is what he puts on the screen. In contrast, I make a different kind of cinema that I think is more European. The Italians have the *commedia dell'arte* or Pirandello, the British George Bernard Shaw, the French a lot of others, even Claudel. All tend toward this relationship: is it life, or is it not? What's good is the attempt to put spectators both inside and out, spurring all of his virtualities. It plays with his thought and sensibilities. The film doesn't present a sort of ready-made; the spectator must produce it himself, alongside the film, and thus becomes active.

JAG: Your films are of diverse lengths, from a few minutes for short films to almost seven hours for *Le Soulier de satin.* Do you think that the cinema is totally free vis-à-vis time?

MO: No, I don't think so. The cinema is not free. I don't think a priori about the problem of duration, whether to do it one way or another. What counts is never to lose one's footing. One should not go off course; it's important to have one's feet on the ground. If I use a writer, I become an interpreter of his work, and what is the interpretation? One might think that one has to do something different in order to express oneself. Interpret means to know, to penetrate, to go inside, not leaving but entering profoundly, seeking to know it as well as possible. I am limited to the work I am filming. I try to show what is inside it; I try not to talk about myself. My work is an interpretation. That's the case of *O Dia do Desespero, Non ou a Vã Glória de Mandar, Amor de Perdição, Francisca, Le Soulier de satin.* It is a total respect for the works. In *Non ou a Vã Glória de Mandar,* there is no fantasy. If I read, "They cut off his hand," it's a question of cutting off his hand, that's it, with no particular emotion, nothing more than what the chronicler said. He is very dry, he says: "They cut off one of his hands, then the other." Americans would cut off his hands with screams and blood. But I do none of that, much to the contrary. If I adapt things, I change them, and they become something else, they don't remain the same. I really like the phrase in the *A Divina Comédia:* "I stick to the facts." There is no need to change facts. Rather, it is necessary to stick to what the writer or historian says. If I want to do something else, then that's truly another story. It is historical fiction, imagined fantasy. The chronicler doesn't matter anymore. One makes people live that one doesn't know, and the work is no more than the fruit of the imagination.

JAG: So you don't worry a priori about the length of the script and the duration of the resulting film?

MO: No, never. I write the screenplay, and it determines a certain position vis-à-vis the subject. For example, for my next film, *Abraham's Valley,* I am working with a book by Agustina Bessa-Luís. I'm the one who suggested that she write the novel. She came to see me, she wanted to work with me on a topic that she felt we could write a screenplay about. I asked here if she wouldn't prefer to write a novel about the subject. I said that it would be better like that, because otherwise there was the risk that I would want to do things one way, and she would want them another way. For the sake of inspiration, it was better for her to do what she wanted and to write the book. Afterwards, I could take the book and come up with my own interpretation. It's much better to make a film based on a novel. She was free to follow her own inspiration, as was I. She accepted and wrote the novel.

Now I'm going to film it. I brought the book with me. I began to write the screenplay in Switzerland, and I have continued here in Paris. I haven't read the whole book, I don't want to know how the book unfolds. I have begun to write the découpage chapter by chapter. It's quite curious because I don't know precisely—I know vaguely, because she told me the main lines of her novel—what's in the book. This method works very well. I don't know how long the film will end up, but I know that it will be a film with a lot of shots and a great rigor of construction. This way of working appeals to me. It comes to me little by little; it's a revelation. The découpage itself that I am now writing is a revelation for me. It's very interesting.

JAG: You rarely work with original screenplays. Why this preference for adaptations?

MO: Before, I wrote a lot of original screenplays; some of them have been published. If we imagine a story as a director, we suddenly begin to write in cinematic terms. That's what I reject. If, on the contrary, I have a book that I must respect, I can't leave it behind. It is necessary to do things from the inside. One is forced to have a much greater rigor, precisely by respecting, according to the specific case, history, a novel, a poem, a biography. . . . *O Dia do Desespero* is not a biography, but it really is about the last days of Camilo Castelo Branco. The words used are those of Camilo. It is very clear what I added. I tried not to introduce any of my own inventions in relation to what happened. For example, Camilo killed himself with a pistol. In the découpage I included a pistol that falls from his hand. But there is no reference to the pistol, no official identification. When the judge interrogates Camilo's wife, he asks her if she saw the pistol, and she responds, "No, I didn't see it." I've been told that Camilo bought a pistol that he always carried. He said that the pistol was his salvation. Since Camilo's wife said that she didn't see the pistol, I decided not to use it at the moment of filming. Why include an object that wasn't part of a certain testimony? If I had included it, it would have been an invention on my part.

JAG: But we know how Camilo Castelo Branco died.

MO: He died without witnesses. He shot himself with a pistol, because he had a hole in his head. Shortly before he killed himself, his doctor came to see him. The doctor is there with his wife, and Camilo asks her to see him out. When they leave, they hear the gunshot. They return to the room, and they discover Camilo slumped in his rocking chair. But there is no question of a pistol. His wife doesn't say if the pistol was there or not, she says nothing. Thus I didn't include it. I put his cigar beside him because he was apparently smoking a cigar. I really like the idea that the cigar remains, but not the pistol.

JAG: How did you come up with the idea of filming *Le Soulier de satin*?

MO: I met Jacques Parsi in Lisbon, we were in the same hotel. He had seen *Benilde*. He introduced himself and spoke of the film with great interest. We talked about frustrated love, and I mentioned Camilo's *Amor de Perdição;* he responded by referring to *The Charterhouse of Parma* and *Le Soulier de satin*. He told me about Prouhèze, who marries Don Camille because she couldn't marry Don Rodrigue. I found that very interesting, and I wanted to read the play. I discovered that the play was connected to Portuguese history, which made me even more interested. Don Rodrigue's spirit is really a Portuguese spirit. The only French figure is Prouhèze; the others are Spanish or Portuguese. The story passes through Portugal during the period in which the country was ruled by the King of Spain. I thus thought about filming it, even though the amplitude of the subject made it a difficult project. At a given moment Jack Lang invited me to make the film as a coproduction. I had the opportunity to film it, and I did.

JAG: Considering its length, the film was quite a challenge.

MO: That's true. I had thought about distributing only the final part. Claudel wrote the last episode first, then the rest. So I thought the final episode had a certain autonomy and that it could constitute the film for the cinema, the rest being limited to restricted distribution or for television. But in truth, the film is more beautiful when one sees the whole thing rather than just the final part. When one reaches the end, it attains its full effect because of the weight of everything that comes before. In France, it was projected everywhere, in Paris as well as the provinces, in the seven-hour version. In Portugal, the film was presented in French because of difficulties with the translation of Claudel. That obviously limited its diffusion. It is very difficult to translate Claudel. His style has a very beautiful musical side that is hard to render in another language. There was a translator who could do it, but he didn't have enough time; another tried but gave up. It was too long and difficult. It requires someone who has a passion for the text and who has a style that approaches Claudel's musicality. *Le Soulier de satin* has never been translated into Portuguese. There is a bad German translation and an English translation with a complete study of the play.

JAG: To finish, could you talk about the play *De Profundis*, which you wrote and directed in 1987 in the Santarcangelo de Romagne festival in Italy?

MO: I started with a short text by Agustina Bessa-Luís, "De Profundis," which is no more than a page long. I really loved the text, and I developed it with the idea of making a film. It's the story of a man who falls in a dry well, far from everything, and who, a prisoner at the bottom of a hole, reflects on many things. Tonino Guerra, the director of the Santarcangelo festival, invited me to direct a play there. I thus thought about transposing my film to the theater. I imagined a glass cylinder to represent the well. It is the only décor, and the public sits around it. The play has only one actor and an accompanying soundtrack. Generally one goes from the theater to the cinema, but this time it was the cinema that moved to the theater. Before going to Italy, I had prepared everything in Lisbon, I had rehearsed everything. A friend helped me when I wasn't there to rehearse with Ruy Furtado, an actor who died during the shooting of *A Divina Comédia*. The play was quite successful. The theater was very full; we had distributed an Italian translation, and almost everyone followed the monologue without difficulty. At the beginning, the lights are completely off; when they come back on, the man has just fallen screaming into the well. The representation begins. At the end, the lights go down again, the actor leaves the well through a trap door and, when the lights come back on, the well is empty. The actor then appears, outside of the well, to greet the public. In Santarcangelo Ruy Furtado was applauded so enthusiastically that he returned to the stage three times, but then he did not respond to further audience calls.

I asked him why he didn't return, and he said, "They were very kind, but I didn't want to abuse the situation." Ruy Furtado was like that, he was a special man who thought that he shouldn't abuse the public. . . .

Recorded in French in Paris in March 1992 (thanks to Jacques Parsi for his linguistic assistance). Translated by Randal Johnson.

An Interview with Manoel de Oliveira

Ruy Gardnier

RUY GARDNIER: I was reading a commemorative volume of *Trafic*, which includes an article of yours. The editors say that they feel guilty since they are French and are unable to find the citation of Molière that you use in "Rethinking the Cinema."[1]

MANOEL DE OLIVEIRA: Three hundred years ago Molière said that language serves both to explain thought and as a portrait of things and people. That's extraordinary. Before him Aristotle said that the soul could not think without images. It's interesting that long before Molière he said the same thing, but in another way. But Descartes, who is also very special, also says something that is very interesting: "What one sees is no less true than what one hears." Our senses are not useless. We can look at an object and think it is smooth, but our sense of touch will tell us if it is really smooth or rough. Of course, our experience offers the first impression, followed by sight, that something we see as smooth continues to be smooth. But it may be proved wrong when one touches the object, which may in fact be rough.

RG: These are the paradoxes that Diderot talked about. . . .

MO: They aren't paradoxes. They are penetrations of our knowledge of human reason and of the senses. The illusion we have that the cinema is movement lies at the heart of its very creation, but that is not its true function as art, or what it became after adding language and sound. It became a synthesis of all the arts. They are not all present at the same time when what one sees is not what one hears, or when what one sees of that which one hears is not what one is seeing. Therefore, if one superimposes an image of that which one hears over an image of what one sees, it becomes confusing and complicates things. But that's not the way it is, they complete each other, with the sound enriching the image. We see two images, or, so to speak, two ideas simultaneously, without interfering with each other.

RG: It's interesting how you seem to use all of the arts. I remember specifically an image of Leonor Silveira carrying a cigarette holder in front of a *clin d'œil* in *Inquietude*, while at the same time posing as a figure, a kind of model; in short, she carries everything: scenography, painting, theater. . . . It seems that the arts don't have to conflict with each other to constitute an art, while the cinema, to affirm itself as a specific art, had to struggle against literature, painting. . . . You, on the contrary, seem to aggregate all of them.

MO: I do, and that's how it should be. In the beginning, since it was silent, the cinema attempted to take its first steps, in the sense of art, as a specific art, wanting to express itself through its own image. Something close to dreams. The cinema was a dream, because dreams have no voice or sound, only images. In order to give a sense of the locomotive's whistle when it was about to depart, the cinema had to film the steam coming out, and we knew it was the whistle. We no longer need that. When it added language and sound, the cinema was enriched, and it left the oneiric for reality. It became much closer to life. There is no art that deludes life as much as the cinema, not even the theater. Not painting, not literature, not abstract art. When you read a book, you are a director, because you are creating images, imagining the face of the actors, their dress, their gait, all of this. You are seeing your own film. And generally when the spectator reads the book before seeing the film, since he has already made his film, the film he sees on the screen doesn't correspond to the one he himself made, so he doesn't like it. But if he didn't read the book and sees the film, he accepts it. Then he'll read the book and see in it the film that he had seen.

RG: I'd like to know how you work with actors, since they all have a distinctive mark in your films.

MO: The critical moment for me is the choice of actors. For the story I have, for the film that I'm going to make, there are a certain number of characters. Characters are fictional; they don't exist. If I make a film about Napoleon, for example, there are several figures of Napoleon, and I'm going to search for someone who looks like him. When they are fictional characters, there is no preexisting figure, and we go for the person who comes closest psychologically and physically to the character. It is a structuring moment for the director, because if he doesn't get it right, everything is ruined. That is, from there on, the actor becomes the character. He is going to give his body, face, voice, gestures, attitudes, and so forth. Therefore, the character died, and now the actor is the character. That's what makes him play the role, because he is the character. Naturally he read a few pages, a book, and he thus interprets things according to what he read and what he feels as the character. And the choice helps, if it is well made. If not, it hinders. I don't like to direct actors in the sense of mise-en-scène, to tell them, "Say it this way or that." No, I like the actor's spontaneity. They speak in accordance to how they feel the character that they are representing feels. I only correct them if I feel that it is exaggerated or insufficient, then I'll ask them to "be stronger" or "be softer." But that's rare. What I do is mark out their movements, telling them to sit here, to sit there, to go in that direction, and so on. These movements give the actor a sense of security. If I don't say anything other than "do it," they feel lost. If I give them some yardsticks, the actor is more comfortable and spontaneity comes out, as does the actor's best performance.

RG: Your work with actors involves a relation of distanciation on nonidentification between the spectator and the character.

MO: I don't want to confuse the spectator with the character. Whether I manage to do so or not, my desire is for the spectator to be active, not passive. I will frequently ask the actor to speak to the camera, or rather to the spectator. The spectator, in turn, can think that's good or bad, can accept it or not, can like it or not. The spectator needs to complete the action he sees in the film. I like to do that and not manipulate the spectator, inducing him to be sentimental and fall in love with the character. There are often films that make the spectator sympathize with an evil character, someone who does bad things but who becomes sympathetic as the film take his defense. At times it is the opposite; they want to get out of their chairs and beat him with a stick. And modern cinema has this tendency, particularly American cinema, to manipulate the spectator, turning him into a plaything, and he leaves the theater as if he had taken drugs.

RG: Your films give a lot of importance to static gestures by actors, just as you take a dynamic and declamatory art from the theater. I believe that you take this static power from painting, from a gesture that may be a synthesis of movements. . . .

MO: I don't take anything from theater or painting. I love painting, but I make paintings with my framing. I don't follow any painter. Of course, I'm influenced by literature, by painting, by music. All of these things influenced and educated me, but I do it in my own way. When I do my painting, I don't want to do in the style of Velázquez or anyone else. I do as I think I should in the way that seems best to me.

RG: A film that impressed me a lot is *A Talking Picture*, your work prior to *O Quinto Império*. In it we see the force of the word, of European languages. Besides the theme of the lack of understanding between East and West, the film develops as a parallel the question of the Portuguese language and the role of Portugal in the European community.

MO: I don't believe that that's what it's about, and not all European languages are there. The film is based above all on Western civilization, Judeo-Christian, Greco-Roman civilization, as well as the Mediterranean character. After the defeat of the invincible armada, the English took control of the seas, which previously belonged to the Peninsula. They took over Western civilization and dominated it for a long time. After the [Second] World War, domination moved to Washington. But the civilization there is still Judeo-Christian, Greco-Roman, and Mediterranean. The strongest contributions, which I wanted to show, are from Greece, Italy, and the Arabs, who spread Greek culture throughout Europe, and the Iberian Peninsula, through the discoveries. More to the north, with England and Holland, is the humanistic part. But what the humanists did in theory, the discoveries did in practice: they discovered numerous countries, established relations with the people there, even married them. Therefore, there was a humanistic expansion in practice. What characterizes the Renaissance is the north with humanism, Italy with the arts, and the Peninsula with the discoveries. *A Talking Picture* speaks of the relationship of this civilization with Arab countries. Western civilization and Western countries were formed in a struggle against Muslims, expelling them from Europe. Now the Muslims are the ones who want to return to Europe, or to the West. There is also the question of terrorism. The Arabs have been on one side and the other, and my new film, about King Sebastian [*O Quinto Império*], includes a myth that is also Arabic, which is that of the Encoberto or Hidden One who will return to combat evil and establish harmony.

RG: The ending of *A Talking Picture* is very apprehensive. There is a fear that both history and coexistence among peoples will be lost. It is an apocalyptic ending.

MO: You're right, it's apocalyptic. But beside that, and perhaps more simply and more profound, is the position of the captain. As you know, the captain is the last one to abandon ship. In the film, when he is already in the lifeboat, he sees that there are still passengers on board, and that they should be there. He is therefore in a very difficult moral position. He should return to save the woman, but it's impossible because it is too late. Besides that, he sees the destruction of his ship, which is his history, his house, his life. He sees the destruction of everything.

RG: It is Mediterranean Europe that is on the ship. . . .

MO: Yes. In the final analysis, it is the world that loses.

RG: Serge Daney said that whenever he saw an image or a shot he would look for what would be the countershot, the element that would be outside but creating tension within the shot. He said that the filmmaker who taught him to think this way was Godard, who has a dialectical or Socratic posture, if you will, putting two sides in conflict. Making an uncommon comparison with your films, I believe that you also bring things into conflict, but where Godard wants to see politics, you try to see history. In your films the dynamic of contrary positions works less in terms of opposites than in terms of accumulation.

MO: In the presentation of his new film, Kiarostami said that tragedy needs a mask.

RG: That's like Nietzche's "Everything that is profound needs a mask."

MO: Right. Here there is confusion between Godard and this phrase. The mask shows what one can't see. In other words, it shows what is behind the mask. In Daney's sense, and I respect him a great deal, as well as that of Godard, the dialectic has a Marxist function, since both have a Marxist tendency. I appreciate both Godard and Serge Daney, but in this particular case I prefer Nietzsche, who is much richer: "Tragedy is behind the mask." It is not what one sees, it is what the mask shows, something that is not visible. If Aristotle says that one cannot think without an image, when we see an image, we see a thought through it. The image is a mask that gives us the thought. We invert the position. When the captain in *A Talking Picture* sees his house explode, he sees a thought: "I should be there. I am morally lacking." On the other hand, he also sees and hears the destruction of his ship, which was his life, which he governed, oriented, and steered against storms and in which he took care of passengers and so forth. It is a mask that leads not to the ship but to the house; not to the house but to the city; not to the city but to the country; not to the country but to the continent; not to the continent but to the world.

RG: You dealt with Sebastianism in *Non ou a Vã Glória de Mandar.* Is there any relationship with *O Quinto Império,* or is it something completely different?

MO: It's something else. *O Quinto Império* was a very difficult film to make because it is taken from a very rich dramatic play. In it, masks are everything. Behind the dialogues is a whole mythical universe, the whole idea of the Fifth Empire, the idea of power that finds harmony. The region encountered another region, the country encountered another country in order to encounter a universal world, which is the myth of the Fifth Empire.

Recorded on 29 October 2004 in São Paulo. Translated by Randal Johnson.

1. Manoel de Oliveira, "Repenser le cinéma," *Trafic* 50 (Summer 2004): 37–42.

Features

Aniki-Bóbó (1942)
Production: António Lopes Ribeiro
Distribution: Lisboa Filme, Exclusivos Triunfo
Director: Manoel de Oliveira
Screenplay: Manoel de Oliveira, based on the short story "Meninos
    Milionários" by João Rodrigues de Freitas
Photography: António Mendes
Editor: Vieira de Sousa
Music: Jaime Silva Filho
Cast: Nascimento Fernandes (shopkeeper), Fernanda Matos (Teresinha),
    Horácio Silva (Carlitos), António Santos (Eduardinho), António Morais
    Soares (Pistarim), Feliciano David (Pompeu), Manuel de Sousa
    ("Philosopher"), António Pereira (Batatinhas), Américo Botelho (Estrelas),
    Rafael Mota (Rafael), Vital dos Santos (teacher), Manuel de Azevedo
    (street singer), António Palma (customer), Armando Pedro (clerk), Pinto
    Rodrigues (policeman)
Black and white; 35mm
70 min.

O Acto da Primavera (Rite of spring; 1963)
Production: Manoel de Oliveira
Distribution: Filmes Lusomundo
Director: Manoel de Oliveira
Screenplay: Manoel de Oliveira, based on *Auto da Paixão*, by Francisco Vaz
    de Guimarães
Photography: Manoel de Oliveira
Editor: Manoel de Oliveira
Cast: Nicolau Nunes da Silva (Christ), Ermelinda Pires (Nossa Senhora),
    Maria Madalena (Madalena), Luís de Sousa (accuser), Francisco Luís
    (Pilate), Renato Palhares (Caifás), Germando Carneiro (Judas), José

Fonseca (spy), Justiniano Alves (Herod), João Miranda (Peter), João Luís (John), Manuel Criado (the devil), and the inhabitants of Curalha, Trás-os-Montes
Color; 35 mm
90 min.

O Passado e o Presente (The past and the present; 1971)
Production: Manoel de Oliveira, Centro Português de Cinema
Distribution: Filmes Lusomundo
Director: Manoel de Oliveira
Screenplay: Manoel de Oliveira and Vicente Sanches, based on the play by Vicente Sanches
Photography: Acácio de Almeida
Editor: Manoel de Oliveira
Music: João Paes
Cast: Maria de Saisset (Vanda), Manuela de Freitas (Noémia), Bárbara Vieira (Angélica), Alberto Inácio (Ricardo/Daniel), Pedro Pinheiro (Firmino), António Machado (Maurício), Duarte de Almeida (Honório), José Martinho (Fernando), Alberto Branco (doctor), Guilhermina Pereira (maid), Agostinho Alves (gardener), Pedre Efe (chauffeur), Carlos de Sousa (priest), Cândida Lacerda (woman in the cemetery), António Beringela
Color; 35mm
117 min.

Benilde ou a Virgem-Mãe (Benilde or the Virgin-Mother; 1975)
Production: Tobis Portuguesa, Centro Português de Cinema
Distribution: Filmes Lusomundo, V. O. Filmes
Director: Manoel de Oliveira
Screenplay: Manoel de Oliveira, based on the play by José Régio
Photography: Elso Roque
Editor: Manoel de Oliveira
Music: João Paes
Cast: Maria Amélia Aranda (Benilde), Jorge Rolla (Eduardo), Varela Silva (Benilde's father), Glória de Matos (Eduardo's mother), Maria Barroso (Genoveva), Augusto Figueiredo (Father Cristóvão), Jacinto Ramos (Dr. Fabrício)
Color, 35mm
106 min.

Amor de Perdição (Doomed love; 1978)
Production: Instituto Português de Cinema, Centro Português de Cinema,
Radiotelevisão Portuguesa, Cinequipa, Tobis Portuguesa
Distribution: V. O. Filmes, Ver Filmes
Director: Manoel de Oliveira
Screenplay: Manoel de Oliveira, based on the novel by Camilo Castelo
Branco
Photography: Manoel Costa e Silva
Editor: Solveig Nordlund
Music: João Paes
Cast: António Sequeira Lopes (Simão Botelho), Cristina Hauser (Teresa
de Albuquerque), Elsa Wallenkamp (Mariana), António J. Costa (João
da Cruz), Henrique Viana (Tadeu de Albuquerque), Maria Dulce (Rita
Caldeirão), Ruy Furtado (Domingos Botelho), Ricardo Pais (Baltasar
Coutinho), Maria Barroso (Abadessa de Monchique), Adelaide João
(Madre Prioresa), Duarte de Almeida (ship captain), Lia Gama (nun),
Manuela de Freitas (nun), Vanda Franca (Baltasar's sister), Henrique
Espírito Santos (bishop)
Color, 16mm
262 min.

Francisca (1981)
Production: V. O. Filmes
Distribution: Rank Filmes de Portugal
Director: Manoel de Oliveira
Screenplay: Manoel de Oliveira, based on Agustina Bessa-Luís's novel *Fanny
Owen*
Photography: Elso Roque
Editor: Monique Rutler
Music: João Paes
Cast: Teresa Meneses (Francisca), Diogo Dória (José Augusto Pinto de
Magalhães), Mário Barroso (Camilo Castelo Branco), Rui Mendes (Manuel
Negrão), Paulo Rocha (doctor), Sílvia Rato (Maria Owen), Glória de Matos
(Rita Owen), António Caldeira Pires (José de Melo), Alexandre Brandão
de Melo (Raimundo), Lia Gama (Josefa), Teresa Madruga (Franzina), João
Guedes (Marques), Cecília Guimarães (Judite), Nuno Carinhas (Marcelino
de Matos), Laura Soveral (Senhora Rocha Pinto), Eduardo Viana (Vieira
de Castro), José Wallenstein (Hugo Owen), Manuela de Freitas (Raquel),
Adelaide João (Clotilde), Manuel Dias da Silva (Vicente), Duarte de
Almeida, Isabel de Castro, Castro Manuel
Color, 35mm
167 min.

Visita ou Memórias e Confissões (Visit or memories and confessions; 1982)
Production: Cineastas Associados
Director: Manoel de Oliveira
Screenplay: Manoel de Oliveira
Photography: Elso Roque
Editor: Manoel de Oliveira, Ana Luísa Guimaraes
Cast: Manoel de Oliveira (himself), Maria Isabel de Oliveira (herself),
    Urbano Tavares Rodrigues (himself)
Color, 35mm
68 min.
(To be screened only after the director's death.)

Le Soulier de satin (The satin slipper; 1985)
Production: Metro e Tal, Les Films du Passage
Distribution: Forum Distribution, Cannon International
Director: Manoel de Oliveira
Screenplay: Manoel de Oliveira, based on the play by Paul Claudel
Photography: Elso Roque
Editors: Jeanine Verneau, Jeanine Martin
Music: João Paes
Cast: Luís Miguel Cintra (Dom Rodrigue, Jesuit), Patricia Barzyk (Doña
    Prouhèze), Anne Cosigny (Marie Sept-Epées), Jean-Pierre Bernard (D.
    Camille), Anne Gautier (Doña Musique), Franck Oger (D. Pélage), Jean
    Badin (D. Balthazar), Manuela de Freitas (Doña Isabel), Henri Serre (first
    king), Jean-Yves Berteloot (second king), Catherine Jarret (first actress),
    Anny Romand (second actress), Isabelle Weingarten (guardian angel),
    Denise Gence (Road to Santiago), Marie-Christine Barrault (the moon),
    Maria Barroso (voice of the angels), Marthe Moudiki-Moreau (Jobarbara),
    Bernard Alane (Vice King of Naples), Yann Roussell (Chinese man), Diogo
    Dória (Almagro)
Color, 16mm/35mm
400 min.

Mon Cas (My case; 1986)
Production: Filmargem, Les Films du Passage, SETE
Distribution: Distribuidores Reunidos
Director: Manoel de Oliveira
Screenplay: Manoel de Oliveira, based on José Régio's *O Meu Caso* and the
    Book of Job
Photography: Mário Barroso
Editors: Manoel de Oliveira, Rudolfo Wedeles
Music: João Paes
Cast: Luís Miguel Cintra (unknown man, Job), Bulle Ogier (actress, Job's

wife), Axel Bougousslavsky (theater employee, Elifaz), Fred Personne (author, Bildad), Wladimir Ivanovsky (first spectator, Zofar), Gregoire Osterman (second spectator, Eliú), Heloise Mignot (second actress) Voice: Henri Serre
Color/black and white, 35mm
88 min.

Os Canibais (The cannibals; 1988)
Production: Filmargem, Gemini Films, La Sept (France)
Distribution: Lusomundo
Director: Manoel de Oliveira
Screenplay: Manoel de Oliveira, based on the novella by Álvaro do Carvalhal
Photography: Mário Barroso
Editors: Manoel de Oliveira, Sabine Franel
Music: João Paes
Cast: Luís Miguel Cintra (Viscount of Aveleda), Diogo Dória (D. João), Leonor Silveira (Margarida), Oliveira Lopes (Iago, the narrator), Pedro Teixeira da Silva (Niccolo), Joel Costa (Urbano Solar Sr.), Rogério Samora (Peralta), Rogério Vieira (magistrate), António Loja Neves (baron), Glória de Matos, Cândido Ferreira, José Manuel Mendes, Teresa Corte Real
Voices: Vaz de Carvalho (Viscount of Aveleda), Carlos Guilhermo (D. João), Filomena Amaro (Margarida), António Silva (Peralta), Carlos Fonseca (magistrate), Luís Madureira (baron), Ana Paula Russo for Glória de Matos, Female Choir of the Gulbenkian Orchestra
Color, 35mm
99 min.

Non ou a Vã Glória de Mandar (No or the vain glory of command; 1990)
Production: Madragoa Filmes, Tornasol Films (Spain), Gemini Films, SGGC Films (France)
Distribution: Madragoa Filmes
Director: Manoel de Oliveira
Screenplay: Manoel de Oliveira
Photography: Elso Roque
Editors: Manoel de Oliveira, Sabine Franel
Music: Alejandro Masso
Cast: Luís Miguel Cintra (Lieutenant Cabrita, Viriato, Alexandre Moreira, D. João de Portugal), Diogo Dória (Manuel, Lusitanian warrior, cousin of D. João of Portugal), Luís Lucas (Corporal Brito, Lusitanian warrior, nobleman in Alcácer), Miguel Guilherme (Salvador, Lusitanian warrior, soldier in Alcácer), António Sequeira Lopes (soldier, Lusitanian warrior, soldier in Alcácer), Carlos Gomes (Pedro, soldier in Alcácer), Mateus Lorena (D. Sebastian), Lola Forner (Princess D. Isabel), Raul Fraire

(D. Afonso), Rui de Carvalho (Priest), Teresa Meneses (Diana), Leonor
Silveira (Venus), Catarina Furtado (nymph), Paulo Matos (radio operator,
Vasco da Gama), Luís Mascarenhas (D. Afonso V), Duarte de Almeida
(Baron of Alvito), José Ramos (Frey Fernando), Joaquim Cachepe
(doctor), António Lupi, André Gago, Pepe Ruiz, Angel Gomez, Salvador
Martos, Mateus Cardoso, Altino Almeida, Jaime Silva
Color, 35mm
111 min.

A Divina Comédia (The divine comedy; 1991)
Production: Madragoa Filmes, Gemini Films, 2001 Audiovisuel (France)
Distribution: Atalanta Filmes
Director: Manoel de Oliveira
Screenplay: Manoel de Oliveira
Photography: Ivan Kozelka
Editors: Manoel de Oliveira, Valérie Loiseleux
Cast: Maria de Medeiros (Sonya), Luís Miguel Cintra (prophet), Miguel
Guilherme (Raskolnikov), Mário Viegas (philosopher), Leonor Silveira
(Eve), Diogo Dória (Ivan), Paulo Matos (Jesus), José Wallenstein
(Alyosha), Ruy Furtado (director), Carlos Gomes (Adam), Luís Lima
Barreto (Pharisee), Miguel Yeco (Lazarus), Júlia Buísel (Maria), Laura
Soveral (Elena Ivanovna), Cremilda Gil (Isabel Ivanovna), Maria João Pires
(Marta), Manoel de Oliveira (director), João Romão (first nurse), Nuno
Melo (second nurse)
Color, 35mm
141 min.

O Dia do Desespero (Day of despair; 1992)
Production: Madragoa Filmes, Gemini Filmes (France)
Distribution: Atalanta Filmes
Director: Manoel de Oliveira
Screenplay: Manoel de Oliveira
Photography: Mário Barroso
Editors: Manoel de Oliveira, Valérie Loiseleux
Cast: Teresa Madruga (Ana Plácido), Mário Barroso (Camilo Castelo Branco),
Luís Miguel Cintra (Freitas Fortuna), Diogo Dória (Dr. Edmundo
Magalhaes), Nuno Melo, José Maria Vaz da Silva, Dina Tereno, David
Ferreira Dias
Color, 35mm
75 min.

Vale Abraão (Abraham's valley; 1993)
Production: Madragoa Filmes, Gemini Films (France), Light Night
(Switzerland)
Distribution: Atalanta Filmes
Director: Manoel de Oliveira
Screenplay: Manoel de Oliveira, based on the novel by Agustina Bessa-Luís
Photography: Mário Barroso
Editors: Manoel de Oliveira, Valérie Loiseleux
Cast: Leonor Silveira (Ema Cardeano Paiva), Luís Miguel Cintra (Carlos de
Paiva), Cécile Sanz de Alba (the young Ema), Rui de Carvalho (Paulino
Cardeano), Glória de Matos (Maria do Loreto), Luís Lima Barreto (Pedro
Lumiares), João Perry (Pedro Dossem), Diogo Dória (Fernando Osório),
Isabel Ruth (Ritinha), Micheline Larpin (Simona), José Pinto (Caires),
Filipe Cochofel (Fortunato), António Reis (Semblano), Dina Treno
(Branca), Dalila Carmo e Sousa (Marina), Laura Soveral (Tia Augusta),
António Wagner (Baltasar), Nuno Vieira de Almeida (Nelson), Joaquim
Nogueira (Narciso), Sofia Alves (Lolota), Beatriz Batarda (Luisona as a
girl), Isabel de Castro (Mana Melo), Júlia Buísel (second Mana Melo),
Monique Dodd (Chelinha), Miguel Guilherme (motorcyclist)
Color, 35mm
187 min.

A Caixa (The box; 1994)
Production: Madragoa Filmes, Gemini Filmes (France), La Sept (France)
Distribution: Atalanta Filmes
Director: Manoel de Oliveira
Screenplay: Manoel de Oliveira, based on the play by Prista Monteiro
Photography: Mário Barroso
Editors: Manoel de Oliveira, Valérie Loiseleux
Cast: Luís Miguel Cintra (blind man), Isabel Ruth (vendor), Glicínia Quartin
(old woman), Rui de Carvalho (tavern owner), Beatriz Batarda (blind man's
daughter), Filipe Cochofel (blind man's son-in-law), Diogo Dória (friend),
Sofia Alves (prostitute), Miguel Guilherme (customer), António Fonseca
(second customer), Rogério Samora (third customer), Duarte Costa (guitar
player), Paula Seabra (pregnant woman), Tino Henriques (grandson),
Gilberto Gonçalves (crippled man), Rogério Vieira (night watchman), Júlia
Buísel (naïf painter), Sharon Ahrens (first tourist), Marsha Smith (second
tourist), Joel Ferreira (friend of the grandson), Susan Alves (girl), Duarte
de Almeida (second blind man), João Gustavo (boy), José Wallenstein
(companion), Mário Barroso (companion), Carla Brígida (neighbor)
Color, 35mm
93 min.

O Convento (The convent; 1995)
Production: Madragoa Filmes, Gemini Filmes (France), La Sept (France),
    with the participation of the Secretaria de Estado da Cultura and Canal+
Distribution: Atalanta Filmes
Director: Manoel de Oliveira
Screenplay: Manoel de Oliveira, inspired by Agustina Bessa-Luís's novel *As
    Terras do Risco*
Photography: Mário Barroso
Editors: Manoel de Oliveira, Valerie Loiseleux
Cast: Catherine Deneuve (Hélène), John Malkovich (Michael Padovic), Luís
    Miguel Cintra (Baltar), Leonor Silveira (Piedade), Duarte de Almeida
    (Baltazar), Heloísa Miranda (Berta), Gilberto Gonçalves (fisherman)
Color, 35mm
91 min.

Party (1996)
Production: Madragoa Filmes, Gemini Films (France)
Distribution: Atalanta Filmes
Director: Manoel de Oliveira
Screenplay: Manoel de Oliveira, Agustina Bessa-Luís
Photography: Renato Berta
Editors: Manoel de Oliveira, Valérie Loiseleux
Cast: Michel Piccoli (Michel), Irene Pappas (Irene), Leonor Silveira
    (Leonor), Rogério Samora (Rogério), Sofia Alves (Dame)
Color, 35mm
91 min.

Viagem ao Princípio do Mundo (Voyage to the beginning of the world; 1997)
Production: Madragoa Filmes, Gemini Films (France)
Distribution: Atalanta Filmes
Director: Manoel de Oliveira
Screenplay: Manoel de Oliveira
Photography: Renato Berta
Editor: Valérie Loiseleux
Music: Emanuel Nunes
Cast: Marcello Mastroianni (Manoel), Leonor Silveira (Judite), Diogo Dória
    (Duarte), Jean-Yves Gauthier (Afonso), Isabel de Castro (Maria Afonso),
    José Pinto (José Afonso), Cécile Sanz de Alba (Cristina), Isabel Ruth (Olga)
Color, 35mm
95 min.

Inquietude (Disquiet; 1998)
Production: Madragoa Filmes, Gemini Films (France), Light Night
    (Switzerland), Wanda Films (Espanha)
Distribution: Atalanta Filmes
Director: Manoel de Oliveira
Screenplay: Manoel de Oliveira, based on *Os Imortais,* by Helder Prista
    Monteiro, "Suzy," by António Patrício, and *A Mãe de um Rio,* by Agustina
    Bessa-Luís
Photography: Renato Berta
Editor: Valérie Loiseleux
Music: Serge Rachmaninov, Aristide Bruant, traditional Greek songs
Cast: "Os Imortais": José Pinto (the father), Luís Miguel Cintra (the son),
    Isabel Ruth (Marta), Leonor Araújo (girl), Afonso Araújo (boy); "Suzy":
    Leonor Silveira (Suzy), Rita Blanco (Gabi), Diogo Dória (the young man),
    David Cardoso (the friend), António Reis (the count), Alexandre Melo
    (companion), Isabel de Oliveira and Manoel de Oliveira (tango dancers),
    Júlia Buísel (cocotte); "The Mother of the River": Irene Pappas (the
    Mother of the River), Leonor Baldaque (Fisalina), Ricardo Trepa (Fisalina's
    boyfriend), Adelaide Teixeira (stepmother), Fernando Bento (Fisalina's
    father), Marco Ferreira (first brother), André Pacheco (second brother)
Color, 35mm
114 min.

La Lettre (The letter; 1999)
Production: Madragoa Filmes, Radiotelevisão Portuguesa/RTP, Gemini Films
    (France), Walda Films (Spain)
Distribution: Atalanta Filmes
Director: Manoel de Oliveira
Screenplay: Manoel de Oliveira, based freely on Madame de Lafayette's *La*
    Princesse de Clèves
Photography: Emmanuel Machuel
Editors: Valérie Loiseleux, Catherine Krassovsky
Music: Pedro Abrunhosa, Maria João Pires
Cast: Chiara Mastroianni (Madame de Clèves), Antoine Chappey (Jacques
    de Clèves), Pedro Abrunhosa (himself), Leonor Silveira (nun), Françoise
    Fabian (Madame de Chartres), Luís Miguel Cintra (Mr. da Silva), Anny
    Romand (Madame da Silva), Stanislas Merhar (Françoise de Guise), Maria
    João Pires (herself), Claude de Leveque (Madame de Chartres's doctor),
    Alain Guillo (jewelry store owner), Jean-Loup Wolf (doctor), Ricardo Trepa
    (drugged beggar), Alexandre Manaia (Abrunhosa's musician), Marianne
    Bey Zave (Madame de Chartres's maid), Marcel Terroux (gardener),
    Claude Sempere (voice of television announcer)
Color, 35mm
100 min.

Palavra e Utopia (Word and Utopia; 2000)
Production: Madragoa Filmes, Radiotelevisão Portuguesa/RTP, Gemini Films
    (France), Walda Films (Spain), Plateau Produções (Brazil)
Distribution: Atalanta Filmes
Director: Manoel de Oliveira
Screenplay: Manoel de Oliveira
Photography: Renato Berta
Editors: Valérie Loiseleux, Catherine Krassovsky
Cast: Ricardo Trepa (António Vieira as a young man), Luís Miguel Cintra
    (António Vieira as an adult), Lima Duarte (mature António Vieira), Leonor
    Silveira (Queen Cristina of Sweden), Renato Di Carmine (Father Jeronimo
    Cattaneo), Miguel Guilherme (Father José Soares), Canto e Castro
    (governor), Diogo Dória (chief inquisitor), Paulo Mattos (notary), António
    Reis (accuser), Rogério Vieira (King D. João IV), Ronaldo Bonacchi
    (Father Bonucci), Rogério Samora (provincial), José Pinto (provincial),
    Luís Lima Barreto (Father Pacheco), Duarte de Almeida (the Pope), José
    Manuel Mendes (inquisitor), Rui Luís (Nuncio)
Color, 35mm
132 min.

Je Rentre à la Maison (I'm going home; 2001)
Production: Madragoa Filmes, Gemini Films (France), France 2 Cinéma
    (France)
Distribution: Atalanta Filmes
Director: Manoel de Oliveira
Screenplay: Manoel de Oliveira
Photography: Sabine Lancelin
Editor: Valérie Loiseleux
Music: Excerpts from Chopin, Wagner, Leo Ferré, and others
Cast: Michel Piccoli (Gilbert Valence), Catherine Deneuve (Marguerite),
    John Malkovich (director), Leonor Baldaque (Sylvia), Leonor Silveira
    (Marie), Isabel Ruth (woman with the milk), Antoine Chappey (George),
    Ricardo Trepa (guard), Jean-Michel Arnold (doctor), Marcel Bozonnet
    (Stéphane), Adrien de Van (Ferdinand), Sylvie Testud (Ariel), Daniel Jean
    (Caliban), Jacques Parsi (agent's friend), Jean Koeltgen (Serge), Mauricette
    Gourdon (Guilhermine), Joel Chicot (first servant), Bruno Guillot (thief),
    Cristian Ameri (second servant), Robert Daunay (Haines), Andre Wale
    (Stephen)
Color, 35mm
90 min.

Porto da Minha Infância (Porto of my childhood; 2001)
Production: Madragoa Filmes, Radiotelevisão Portuguesa/RTP
Distribution: Atalanta Filmes
Director: Manoel de Oliveira
Screenplay: Manoel de Oliveira
Photography: Emmanuel Machuel
Editor: Valérie Loiseleux
Cast: Ricardo Trepa (Manoel de Oliveira as a young man), Jorge Trepa
(Manoel de Oliveira as an adolescent), Rogério Samora, Agustina Bessa-
Luís, José Wallenstein, Maria de Medeiros, Leonor Silveira, Leonor
Baldaque, Duarte de Almeida, Peter Rudel
Color, 35mm
62 min.

O Princípio da Incerteza (The uncertainty principle; 2002)
Production: Gemini Films (Paris), Madragoa Filmes (Lisbon), Radiotelevisão
Portuguesa (RTP)
Distribution: Madragoa Filmes, Gemini Films
Director: Manoel de Oliveira
Screenplay: Júlia Buisel, António Costa, Manoel de Oliveira, and Jacques
Parsi, based on the novel by Agustina Bessa-Luís
Photography: Renato Berta
Editors: Manoel de Oliveira, Catherine Krassovsky
Cast: Leonor Baldaque (Camila), Leonor Silveira (Vanessa), Isabel Ruth
(Celsa), Ricardo Trepa (José Luciano), Ivo Canelas (António Clara),
Luís Miguel Cintra (Daniel Roper), José Manuel Mendes (Torcato
Roper), Cecília Guimaraes (Rutinha), Duarte de Almeida (Mr. Ferreira),
Júlia Buisel (Aunt Tofi), Diogo Dória (policeman), António Fonseca
(policeman), Father João Marques (priest), Carmen Santos (Joana)
Color, 35mm
133 min.

Um Filme Falado (A talking picture; 2003)
Production: Madragoa, Gemini, Mikado, France 2 Cinema
Distribution: Gemini Films
Director: Manoel de Oliveira
Screenplay: Manoel de Oliveira
Photography: Emmanuel Machuel
Editor: Valérie Loiseleux
Cast: Leonor Silveira (Rosa Maria), Catherine Deneuve (Delfine), Irene
Pappas (Helena), Stefania Sandrelli (Francesca), John Malkovich (Captain
John Walesa), Filipa de Almeida (Maria Joana), Luís Miguel Cintra
(Portuguese actor), Michel Lubrano de Sbaraglione (fisherman), François

da Silva (fisherman's customer), Nikos Hatzopoulos (Orthodox priest), Antònio Ferraiolo (guide in Pompeii), Alparslan Salt (guide at Hagia Sophia), Ricardo Trepa (official), David Cardoso (official), Júlia Buísel (Delfine's friend)
Color, 35 mm
96 min.

O Quinto Império: Ontem como Hoje (The Fifth Empire: Yesterday as today; 2004)
Production: Paulo Branco, Madragoa Filmes, Gemini Filmes
Distribution: Madragoa Filmes
Director: Manoel de Oliveira
Screenplay: Manoel de Oliveira, based on the play *El-Rei Sebastião,* by José Régio
Historical Advisor: P. João Marques
Photography: Sabine Lancelin
Editor: Valérie Loiseleux
Music: Carlos Paredes
Cast: Ricardo Trepa (King Sebastian), Luís Miguel Cintra (Simão, the Holy Cobbler), Glória de Matos (Queen Catarina), Miguel Guilherme (jester), David Almeida (jester), Ruy de Carvalho (counselor), José Manuel Mendes (counselor), Luís Lima Barreto (counselor), Rogério Samora, José Wallenstein, Filipe Cochofel, Nuno M. Cardoso, Carlos Gomes, Ramón Martínez (noblemen)
Color, 35 mm
127 min.

Espelho Mágico (Magic mirror; 2005)
Production: Miguel Cadilhe, Filbox
Distribution: Lusomundo
Director: Manoel de Oliveira
Screenplay: Manoel de Oliveira, based on the novel *O Princípio da Incerteza: A Alma dos Ricos,* by Agustina Bessa-Luís
Photography: Renato Berta
Editor: Valérie Loiscleux
Sound editor: Mikael Barre
Cast: Leonor Silveira (Alfreda), Ricardo Trepa (José Luciano), Luís Miguel Cintra (Filipe Quinta), Leonor Baldaque (Vicenta/Abril), Glória de Matos (Nurse Hilda), Isabel Ruth (Celsa Adelaide), Adelaide Texeira (Queta), Diogo Dória (comissary), José Wallenstein (Américo), Michel Piccoli (Professor Heschel), Lima Duarte (Father Clodel), Father João Marques (Father Feliciano), Marisa Paredes (nun)
Color, 35mm
137 min.

Belle Toujours (2006)
Production: Miguel Cadilhe, Serge Lalou, Filbox, Les Films d'Ici
Distribution: Lusomundo
Director: Manoel de Oliveira
Screenplay: Manoel de Oliveira
Photography: Sabine Lancelin
Editor: Valérie Loiseleux
Sound editor: Mikael Barre
Cast: Michel Piccoli (Henri Husson), Bulle Ogier (Séverine Serizy), Ricardo
Trepa (barman), Leonor Baldaque (young prostitute), Júlia Buisel (old
prostitute)
Color, 35mm
68 min.

Shorts and Documentaries

"Douro, Faina Fluvial" (Labor on the Douro; 1931)
Production: Manoel de Oliveira
Distribution: Agência Cinematográfica H. da Costa, Sociedade Portuguesa de
Actualidades Cinematográficas
Director: Manoel de Oliveira
Screenplay: Manoel de Oliveira
Photography: António Mendes
Editor: Manoel de Oliveira
Black and white, 35mm
21 min.

"Estátuas de Lisboa" (Lisbon's statues; 1932)
Production: Ulyssea Filme
Distribution: Agência Cinematográfica H. da Costa
Director: Manoel de Oliveira
Photography: Manoel de Oliveira
Black and white, 35 mm
8 min.

"Hulha Branca, Empresa Hidro-Eléctrica do Rio Ave" (White Coal,
Hydroelectric company on the Ave River; 1932)
Production: Hidro-Eléctrica de Portugal
Director: Manoel de Oliveira
Photography: António Mendes
Editor: Manoel de Oliveira
Black and white, 35 mm
7 min.

"Miramar, Praia das Rosas" (Miramar, beach of roses; 1938)
Production: Lisboa Filme
Director: Manoel de Oliveira
Photography: António Mendes
Editor: Manoel de Oliveira
Black and white, 35mm
9 min.

"Portugal Já Faz Automóveis" (Portugal now makes automobiles; 1938)
Production: Lisboa Filme
Distribution: Lisboa Filme
Director: Manoel de Oliveira
Photography: António Mendes
Editor: Manoel de Oliveira
Music: Carlos Calderón
Black and white, 35mm
9 min.

"Famalicão" (1940)
Production: MAOM
Distribution: Lisboa Filme
Director: Manoel de Oliveira
Photography: António Mendes
Editor: Manoel de Oliveira
Music: Jaime Silva Filho
Black and white, 35mm
24 min.

"O Pintor e a Cidade" (The painter and the city; 1956)
Production: Manoel de Oliveira
Distribution: Doperfilme
Director: Manoel de Oliveira
Photography: Manoel de Oliveira
Editor: Manoel de Oliveira
Music: Luís Rodrigues
Color, 35mm
28 min.

"O Pão" (Bread; 1959)
Production: Manoel de Oliveira, sponsored by the Federação Nacional dos
    Industriais de Moagem
Director: Manoel de Oliveira
Screenplay: Manoel de Oliveira

Photography: Manoel de Oliveira
Editor: Manoel de Oliveira
Black and white, 35mm
59 min.

"A Caça" (The hunt; 1963)
Production: Tobis Portuguesa
Distribution: Filmes Lusomundo
Director: Manoel de Oliveira
Screenplay: Manoel de Oliveira
Photography: Manoel de Oliveira
Editor: Manoel de Oliveira
Music: Joly Braga Santos
Cast: António Rodrigues Sousa (José), João Rocha Almeida (Roberto), Albino
    Freitas, Manuel de Sá
Color, 35mm
20 min.

"Villa Verdinho—Uma Aldeia Transmontana" (Villa Verdinho—A village in
    Trás-os-Montes; 1964)
Production: Gaia Filmes
Director: Manoel de Oliveira
Photography: Manoel de Oliveira, Clemente Meneres
Editor: Manoel de Oliveira
Music: José Afonso
Color, 16mm
18 min.

"As Pinturas do meu Irmão Júlio" (My brother Júlio's paintings; 1965)
Production: Manoel de Oliveira
Director: Manoel de Oliveira
Photography: Manoel de Oliveira
Editor: Manoel de Oliveira
Music: Carlos Paredes
Color, 16mm
16 min.

"Lisboa Cultural" (Cultural Lisbon; 1983)
Production: Radiotelevisão Portuguesa/RTP; Trans World Film (Italy), RAI
    (Italy)
Director: Manoel de Oliveira
Photography: Elso Roque
Editor: Ana Luísa Guimaraes

Music: Duarte Costa
Color, 16mm
58 min.

"Nice—À Propos de Jean Vigo" (Nice—About Jean Vigo; 1983)
Production: Institut National de l'Audiovisuel (France)
Distribution: FR3 (France)
Director: Manoel de Oliveira
Photography: Jacques Bouquin
Editors: Jeanine Verneua, Françoise Besnier
Color, 16mm
58 min.

"Simpósio Internacional de Escultura em Pedra—Porto 1985" (International
   Symposium of Stone Sculpture—Porto 1985; 1985)
Production: Metro Filme, Radiotelevisão Portuguesa/RTP
Directors: Manoel de Oliveira, Manuel Casimiro
Screenplay: João Assis Gomes
Photography: João Abel Aboim, Artur Moura
Editors: Leonor Guterres, Celeste Alves
Color, 16mm
60 min.

"A Propósito da Bandeira Nacional" (About the national flag; 1987)
Production: Manoel de Oliveira
Director: Manoel de Oliveira
Screenplay: Pedro Prista Monteiro
Photography: Manoel de Oliveira, Elso Roque
Editor: Manoel de Oliveira
Color, 16mm
7 min.

"En une Poignée de Mains Amies" (In the hold of friendly hands; 1996)
Production: CNRS (France)
Directors: Manoel de Oliveira, Jean Rouch
Screenplay: Manoel de Oliveira
Photography: Jerôme Blumberg
Color, 16mm
25 min.

Bibliography |

Alguns projectos não realizados e outros textos de Manoel de Oliveira. Lisbon: Cinemateca Portuguesa, 1988.

A.M.S. "'Amor de Perdição' em estréia." *Expresso,* 24 November 1978.

Andrade, Joaquim Pedro de. "Cannibalism and Self-Cannibalism." In *Brazilian Cinema.* Ed. Randal Johnson and Robert Stam. New York: Columbia University Press, 1995. 81–83.

Andrade, Sérgio C. *O Porto na História do Cinema.* Porto: Porto Editora, 2002.

"Aniki-Bóbó (1942)." Screening notes. Lisbon: Cinemateca Portuguesa. Ciclo Manoel de Oliveira, 4 October 1981. Textos Cinemateca Portuguesa, folder 5.

De Baecque, Antoine, and Jacques Parsi. *Conversas com Manoel de Oliveira.* Trans. Henrique Cunha. Porto: Campos das Letras, 1999.

Beckett, Samuel. *For to End Again and Other Fizzles.* London: John Calder, 1976.

Bénard da Costa, João. "Benilde ou a Virgem Mãe/1975." Screening notes. Lisbon: Cinemateca Portuguesa. Ciclo Manoel de Oliveira: 90 Anos, 15 December 1998. Textos Cinematica Portuguesa, folder 59.

———. "O cinema é um vício." In *Manoel de Oliveira.* Lisbon: Cinemateca Portuguesa, 1981. 5–12.

———. *Histórias do Cinema.* Lisbon: Imprensa Nacional—Casa da Moeda, 1991.

———. "'Non' ou a Vã Glória de Mandar / 1990." Lisbon: Cinemateca Portuguesa. Ciclo 50 Anos Depois da Estréia de 'Camões,' 26 October 1996. Textos Cinemateca Portuguesa, folder 54.

———. "Party / 1996." Lisbon: Cinemateca Portuguesa. Ciclo Um Mar de Filmes: As Ilhas, 27 March 1998. Textos Cinemateca Portuguesa, folder 57.

———. "Pedra de Toque: O dito Eterno Feminino na Obra de Manoel de Oliveira." *Camões: Revista de Letras e Culturas Lusófonas* 12–13 (January–June 2001): 6–37.

Bessa-Luís, Agustina. *Fanny Owen.* 3d ed. Lisbon: Guimarães Editores, 1979.

———. *A Mãe de um Rio/La Mère d'un fleuve.* Lisbon: Guimarães Editores, 1971.
———. *O Princípio da Incerteza: A Alma dos Ricos.* Lisbon: Guimarães Editores, 2002.
———. *O Princípio da Incerteza: Jóia de Família.* 4th ed. Lisbon: Guimarães Editores, 2001.
———. *As Terras do Risco.* Lisbon: Guimarães Editores, 1994.
——— —. *Vale Abraão.* 4th ed. Lisbon: Guimarães Editores, 1999.
Bouquet, Stéphane. "Histoire de fantômes portugais." *Cahiers du Cinéma* 514 (June 1997): 72–73.
Buisel, Júlia. *Manoel de Oliveira: Fotobiografia.* Lisbon: Livraria Figueirinhas, 2002.
Cabrita, António. "A queda de um anjo: novo filme de Manoel de Oliveira remonta às raízes míticas." *Expresso,* 16 November 2002.
Câmara, Vasco. "Oliveira, o cineasta que faz ver mais em frente." *Público,* 11 September 2004.
Camões, Luís Vaz de. *The Lusiads.* Trans. Landeg White. New York: Oxford University Press, 1997.
Castelo Branco, Camilo. *Doomed Love (A Family Memoir).* Trans. Alice Clemente. Providence, R.I.: Gávea-Brown Publications, 2000.
O Cinema Novo Português, 1960/1974. Lisbon: Cinemateca Portuguesa, 1985.
Clarens, Carlos. "Manoel de Oliveira Interviewed by Carlos Clarens." *Film Comment* 17.3 (May–June 1981): 65–68.
Claudel, Paul. *Le Soulier de satin.* 1929; reprint, Paris: Éditions Gallimard, 2000.
Cohen, Thomas M. *The Fire of Tongues: António Vieira and the Missionary Church in Brazil and Portugal.* Stanford, Calif.: Stanford University Press, 1998.
Costa, Alves. *Breve história do cinema português—1896–1962.* Lisbon: Instituto de Cultura Portuguesa, 1978.
———. "Manoel de Oliveira—fragmentos de um esboço biográfico." In *Manoel de Oliveira.* Lisbon: Cinemateca Portuguesa, 1981. 13–21.
Costa, José Filipe. *O Cinema ao Poder! A revolução do 25 de Abril e as políticas de cinema entre 1974–76: os grupos, instituições, experiências e projectos.* Lisbon: Hugin, 2002.
Costa, José Manuel. "Acto da Primavera (1963)." Lisbon: Cinemateca Portuguesa. Ciclo Manoel de Oliveira em Contexto, 21 November 1988. Textos Cinemateca Portuguesa, folder 39.
———. "O Pão/1959." Lisbon: Cinemateca Portuguesa. Ciclo Manoel de Oliveira: 90 Anos, 18 December 1998. Textos Cinemateca Portuguesa, Pasta 59.
Cruchinho, Fausto. *O Desejo Amoroso em 'Os Canibais' de Manoel de Oliveira.* Porto: Mimesis, 2003.

Dacosta, Fernando. "'A utopia é o caminho para a luz.'" Interview with Manoel de Oliveira. *Visão*, 3 February 2005.

Dreux, Emmanuel. "Party: 'la double constance.'" *L'art du cinéma* 21–23 (Autumn 1998): 145–51.

Duarte, Fernando. "O Passado e o Presente de Manuel de Oliveira." *Celulóide* 15.71 (March 1972): 1–6.

Eisenreich, Pierre. "Irrépressible convoitise." *Positif* 451 (September 1998): 13–15.

Eyny, Yaniv, and A. Zubatov. "Voyage to the End of the World: Manoel de Oliveira's *A Talking Picture*." *Senses of Cinema* 33 (October–December 2004). www.sensesofcinema.com/contents/04/33/a_talking_picture.html.

Ferreira, Manuel Cintra. "Viagem ao Princípio do Mundo/1997." Lisbon: Cinemateca Portuguesa. Ciclo Manoel de Oliveira: 90 Anos, 18 December 1998. Textos Cinemateca Portuguesa, folder 59.

Fonseca, M. S. "Aniki Bóbó / 1942." Lisbon: Cinemateca Portuguesa. Ciclo Manoel de Oliveira em Contexto, 16 November 1988. Textos Cinemateca Portuguesa, folder 39.

———. "A Caça / 1963." Lisbon: Cinemateca Portuguesa. Ciclo Cinema e Real, 27 April 1996. Textos Cinemateca Portuguesa, folder 54.

———. "Mon Cas / 1988." Lisbon: Cinemateca Portuguesa. Ciclo O Culto e o Oculto, 15 October 1993. Textos Cinemateca Portuguesa, folder 49.

Freitas, João Rodrigues de. "Menino milionários na sala de aula." *Presença* 4.2 (August–October 1930): 2–3. Compact facsimile edition, vol. 2. Lisbon: Contexto, 1993.

Gardnier, Ruy. "A Carta." *Contracampo: Revista de Cinema*. www.contracampo .com.br/criticas/acarta.htm.

———. "Inquietude, de Manoel de Oliveira." *Contracampo: Revista de Cinema*. www.contracampo.com.br/criticas/inquietude.htm.

Goethe, Johann Wolfgang von. *Faust I & II*. Ed. and trans. Stuart Atkins. Cambridge, Mass.: Suhrkamp/Insel, 1984.

Granja, Paulo Jorge. "A Comédia à Portuguesa, ou a Máquina de Sonhos a Preto e Branco do Estado Novo." In *O Cinema sob o Olhar de Salazar*. Ed. Luís Reis Torgal. Lisbon: Temas e Debates, 2001. 194–233.

Henriques, Joana Gorjão. "Grande Prémio APE para Agustina Bessa-Luís." *Público*, 21 May 2002.

Holden, Stephen. "'The Letter': An Old-Fashioned Girl, Pining for Perfection." *New York Times*, 28 September 1999.

———. "'Voyage to the Beginning of the World': Fading in a World That Seemed Eternal." *New York Times*, 26 June 1998.

Jousse, Thierry. "Le fil de l'épée." *Cahiers du Cinéma* 433 (June 1990): 22–23.

Lemière, Jacques. "Algumas notas sobre a recepção em França de Manoel de Oliveira." *Camões: Revista de Letras e Culturas Lusófonas* 12–13 (January–June 2001): 116–26.

Lopes, João. *Aniki Bóbó*. Lisbon: Secretaria de Estado da Reforma Educativa, n.d.

———. *História do Cinema Português*. Lisbon: Publicações Europa-America, 1986.

Magalhães, Isabel Allegro de. "Camilo sob o olhar de Agustina: entre a história e a ficção?" In *Camilo Castelo Branco no centenário da morte*. Ed. João Camilo dos Santos. Santa Barbara: Center for Portuguese Studies, University of California at Santa Barbara, 1995. 207–17.

"Manoel de Oliveira." Manuscript. Lisbon: Centro Português de Cinema, ca. 1975.

Manoel de Oliveira. Lisbon: Cinemateca Portuguesa, 1981.

Manoel de Oliveira. Ed. Jacques Parsi with Simona Fina and Roberto Turigliatto. Paris: Centre Georges Pompidou, 2001.

"Manoel de Oliveira: Entrevista." In *Olhares sobre Portugal: Cinema e Antropologia*. Lisbon: Centro de Estudos de Antropologia Social do ISCTE e ABC Cine-Clube, n.d.

Marcorelles, Louis. "Les élans du coeur." *Le Monde*, 16 June 1979, 1, 29.

Matos-Cruz, José de. *Manoel de Oliveira e a Montra das Tentações*. Lisbon: Sociedade Portuguesa de Autores, Publicações Dom Quixote, 1996.

Mattos, Carlos Alberto. "O John Woo das Palavras." *Criticos.com*. 29 July 2002. www.criticos.com.br.

"Os momentos do MOMENTO." Web page. momento.no.sapo.pt/.

Monteiro, Helder Prista. *A Caixa: Peça em Dois Actos*. Lisbon: Moraes Editores, 1981.

———. *Os Imortais*. Lisbon: Sociedade Portuguesa de Autores, 1984.

Monteiro, João César. "O Passado e o Presente: Um Necrofilme de Manoel de Oliveira." In *Morituri et Salutant*. Lisbon: Publicações Culturais Engrenagem; Editora Arcádia, 1974. 33–43.

Neto, Anastácio. "Manoel de Oliveira: o decano do cinema português está de volta." *O Comércio do Porto*, 25 January 2005.

"Oliveira le funambule." *Cahiers du Cinéma* 528 (October 1998): 13.

Oliveira, Manoel de. "Dom Quichote por Manoel de Oliveira." Press book for *O Dia do Desespero*. www.madragoafilmes.pt/odiadodesespero.

———. *Lisbonne Culturelle*. Paris: Éditions Dis Voir, 1985.

———. "'O Meu Caso' no Caso de Régio." In *Régio, Oliveira e o Cinema*. Ed. António Pedro Pita. Vila do Conde: Câmara Municipal de Vila do Conde; Cineclube da Vila do Conde, 1994. 35–36.

———. "Nota de Intenções." *A Divina Comédia* Official Web Site. www.madragoafilmes.pt/adivinacomedia/#.

———. "Parole et cinéma." *Cahiers du Cinéma* 555 (March 2001): 42–45.

Paes, João. "Entre a Sinfonia e a Ópera: A música dos filmes da maturidade de Manoel de Oliveira." *Camões: Revista de Letras e Culturas Lusófonas* 12–13 (January–June 2001): 90–97.

Parsi, Jacques. "Entrevista com o realizador." *Vou para Casa*: Press book. Official Web Site: www.madragoafilmes.pt/vouparacasa/.
———. "Filmographie de Manoel de Oliveira." In *Manoel de Oliveira*. Ed. Jacques Parsi with Simona Fina and Roberto Turigliatto. Paris: Centre Georges Pompidou, 2001. 27–64.
——— [Jacques Passi]. "A trilogia dos amores frustrados." In *Manoel de Oliveira*. Lisbon: Cinemateca Portuguesa, 1981. 71–78.
Pina, Luís de. *História do Cinema Português*. Lisbon: Publicações Europa-América, 1986.
Prédal, René. *Manoel de Oliveira: le texte et l'image*. *L'Avant-Scène Cinéma* 478–79 (January–February 1999).
Régio, José. *Benilde ou a Virgem-Mãe*. 2d ed. Lisbon: Portugália Editora, 1970.
———. *El-Rei Sebastião: Poema Espectacular em Três Actos*. Coimbra: Atlântida, 1949.
———. "O Meu Caso." In *Três Peças em um Acto*. 2d ed. Lisbon: Portugália Editora, 1969.
Régio, Oliveira e o Cinema. Ed. António Pedro Pita. Vila do Conde: Câmara Municipal de Vila do Conde; Cineclube da Vila do Conde, 1994.
Ribeiro, M. Félix. *Filmes, Figuras, e Factos da História do Cinema Português, 1896–1949*. Lisbon: Cinemateca Portuguesa, 1983.
Rollet, Sylvie. "Les affinities electives: Manoel de Oliveira et Camilo Castelo Branco." *Positif* 451 (September 1998): 10–15.
Romney, Jonathan. "Eye Travel." *Sight and Sound* 7 (July 1998): 34–35.
Rosenbaum, Jonathan. "Bright Spots in the Darkness." *Chicago Reader on Film*. www.chireader.com/movies/98best.html.
Saguenail and Regina Guimarães. "Caixa Vazia, Caixa de Surpresas." *Grande Ilusão* 17 (March 1995).
Sanches, Vicente. *O Passado e o Presente*. Comedy in Three Acts. Vila Nova de Famalicão: Edição do Autor, Minerva Printing, 1964.
Shakespeare, William. *The Tempest*. Ed. John F. Andrews. London: Everyman, 1994.
Silva, Rodrigues da. "Oliveira, do melhor." *Jornal de Letras*, 13 November 2002.
Stein, Ellliott. "Manoel de Oliveira and 'Doomed Love.'" *Film Comment* 17.3 (May–June 1981): 61.
Tesson, Charles. "Une Passion." *Cahiers du Cinéma* 326 (July–August 1981): 11–13.
Torres, António Roma. *Cinema Português: Anos Gulbenkian*. Porto: N.p., 1974.
Torres, Eduardo Cintra. "Douro, Faina Manoel." *Público*, 18 March 2002.

Index

RANDAL JOHNSON is professor and former chair of Spanish and Portuguese at the University of California at Los Angeles. He is the author or editor of several books, including *Brazilian Cinema* (with Robert Stam), *The Film Industry in Brazil: Culture and the State,* and *Cinema Novo x 5: Masters of Contemporary Brazilian Film.*

Books in the series Contemporary Film Directors

The University of Illinois Press
is a founding member of the
Association of American University Presses.

———————————————————

Composed in 10/13 New Caledonia
with Helvetica Neue Extended display
by Jim Proefrock
at the University of Illinois Press
Designed by Paula Newcomb
Manufactured by Sheridan Books, Inc.

University of Illinois Press
1325 South Oak Street
Champaign, IL 61820-6903
www.press.uillinois.edu